spring

QUADRILLE

spring

the cookbook   Skye Gyngell

Notes Please use sea salt, freshly ground pepper, and fresh herbs.

I use medium eggs—organic and free-range. Anyone who is pregnant or in a vulnerable health group should avoid recipes using raw or lightly cooked eggs.

Please use unwaxed lemons if the recipe calls for the zest.

Timings are for fan-assisted ovens. If using a conventional oven, turn the setting up by about 25–35°F [15–20°C]. Use an oven thermometer to keep a check on the temperature.

The space

I wanted a space that I could really connect with. It needed to be different from my restaurant at Petersham Nurseries with its tumbledown, natural appeal, but just as beautiful in its own way. I wanted somewhere warm and light filled—high ceilinged and grand, but intimate as well. It took me a year to find it . . . I had all but given up hope when I visited Somerset House in London late one afternoon in March 2013.

I stepped into the former government offices to be greeted by swirly burned orange carpet, vinyl desks, and what looked like huge plastic fly-catchers over the windows. The room was big, certainly, with Greek columns and ornate cornicing, but it felt dark, dismal, and damp. It wasn't love at first sight. A light well in the center of the room caught my eye. It, too, had seen better days—the light from it was smudgy, gray, and cold—though it could be repaired. In the far right corner a mellow, gentle light seeped across the floor from a large Georgian window overlooking the River Thames.

I began to warm to the space; I could see it had potential. That smudgy, broken light well could become a garden—a beautiful little jewel of a garden dropped in from the sky, nestling between the reception area and potential kitchen. It became the focal point of my thoughts.

It was a larger space than I had envisaged, which was a bit scary, but I went ahead anyway and submitted a proposal to Somerset House at the end of that month. It was such an exciting prospect yet I didn't dare build up my hopes—the market is fiercely competitive and this was a site that would appeal to far more experienced restaurateurs than me.

I waited and waited for a response. It was unbearable, as I became increasingly convinced that this was the right space for me—the only space for me. Two months passed by without word, then out of the blue I was invited to a meeting to discuss the proposal. Fortunately, it was well received, as the board at Somerset House were looking for a stand-alone restaurant that wasn't part of a chain. They liked the ideas that I put forward with my team and gave us the go-ahead. I was over the moon. The hard work began in earnest—to turn this neglected, once elegant, room into a joyful space.

appetizers

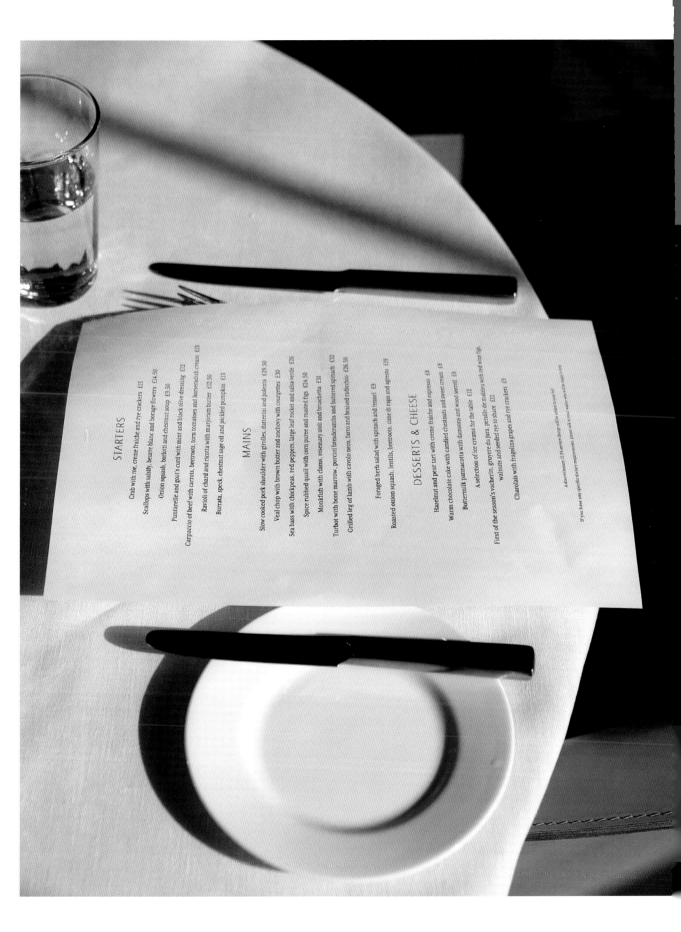

STARTERS

Crab with roe, crème fraîche and rye crackers £15

Scallops with salsify, beurre blanc and borage flowers £14.50

Onion squash, borlotti and chestnut soup £9.50

Puntarelle and goat's curd with mint and black olive dressing £12

Carpaccio of beef with carrots, beetroots, torn tomatoes and horseradish cream £13

Ravioli of chard and ricotta with marjoram butter £12.50

Burrata, speck, chestnut sage oil and pickled pumpkin £13

MAINS

Slow cooked pork shoulder with girolles, datterini and polenta £29.50

Veal chop with brown butter and anchovy with courgettes £30

Sea bass with chickpeas, red peppers, large leaf rocket and salsa verde £26

Spice rubbed quail with corn puree and roasted figs £24.50

Monkfish with clams, rosemary aioli and bruschetta £31

Turbot with bone marrow, porcini breadcrumbs and buttered spinach £32

Grilled leg of lamb with cavolo nero, farro and braised radicchio £26.50

Foraged herb salad with spinach and fennel £9

Roasted onion squash, lentils, beetroots, cime di rapa and agretto £19

DESSERTS & CHEESE

Hazelnut and pear tart with crème fraîche and espresso £8

Warm chocolate cake with candied chestnuts and sweet cream £8

Buttermilk pannacotta with damsons and wood sorrel £8

A selection of ice creams for the table £12

First of the season's vacherin, gruyere du jura, persille de malzieu with red wine figs,
walnuts and seeded rye to share £12

Charolais with fragolina grapes and rye crackers £9

A discretionary 12.5% service charge will be added to your bill

If you have any specific dietary requirements, please talk to your waiter who will be happy to help

Asparagus with crème fraîche and Parmesan

Rich, creamy, and light as air—this is a really nice, simple way to serve asparagus. During its season, I like to eat local asparagus whenever I can. Use a mixture of white and green if possible—the contrasting colors and subtly different flavors are great together. Borage is not so easy to find in stores but if, like me, you grow the herb in your garden, scatter a few flowers over the top just before serving.

Start with the sauce. Bring a large pot of water to a boil and add a generous pinch of salt. Break the eggs into a bowl that fits snugly on top of the pan and add a pinch of salt. Set the bowl over the pan of boiling water, making sure the base is not in contact with the water, and whisk the eggs until smooth. Add the crème fraîche and whisk continuously until the sauce has slightly thickened; it will become thinner at first, then thicken and almost double in volume.

Remove the bowl from the pan. Add the grated Parmesan and season with salt and pepper to taste. Stir well to combine and set aside while you cook the asparagus.

Break off and discard the woody ends from the base of the asparagus stalks. Drop the asparagus spears into the pan of boiling water and cook about 1 minute or until the asparagus is just tender to the bite. Using tongs, remove the asparagus from the water and drain well, then dress with the olive oil and arrange on warm plates.

Set the bowl of sauce back over the pan and heat 1 minute to ensure it is warm, then spoon generously over the asparagus. Finish with the borage flowers, if you have them, or chervil or chives.

Serves 4

About 20 to 30 asparagus spears

1 ½ Tbsp mild-tasting extra virgin olive oil

Sea salt and freshly ground black pepper

For the sauce

2 organic free-range eggs

⅝ cup [150 ml] crème fraîche

⅔ cup [50 g] Parmesan, freshly grated

A scattering of borage flowers (or chervil or chives), to finish

Eggs, anchovies, celery heart, and radishes

I can hardly call this a recipe, more a gathering of a few of my favorite
things on a plate. I love anchovies and never tire of them. A staple in my
storecupboard, I eat them just as they are—on good bread with lots
of unsalted butter—and they season so many of the dishes I cook.
Here, their saltiness cuts the richness of boiled eggs, and the cool, clean
crunch of celery heart and radishes add a refreshing contrast. Tarragon,
a much underused herb, marries the flavors beautifully.

Serves 4

4 medium or large organic
free-range eggs, at room
temperature

8 to 12 inner celery stalks
(the paler stalks around the
heart are sweeter and gentler
in taste)

A bunch of radishes

A little extra virgin olive oil,
to drizzle

A few tarragon sprigs

12 anchovy fillets (preferably
Ortiz)

12 black olives

4 chervil or parsley sprigs

Sea salt and freshly ground
black pepper

Bring a pan of water to a boil. Carefully lower the eggs into
the pan and boil 5 minutes (or 6 minutes if the eggs are large).
Remove them from the pan and run under cold water to
prevent further cooking.

Wash and trim the celery stalks, retaining the leaves. Wash
and trim the radishes, leaving a tuft of stalk attached. Season
the celery and radishes lightly with salt and pepper and
drizzle with a little olive oil.

Peel the eggs, slice them in half lengthwise, and arrange on
large individual plates with the celery and radishes. Arrange
the tarragon, anchovies, and olives on the plates and finish
with the chervil or parsley. Serve with good bread and butter.

Carpaccio of wild salmon with pickled green tomatoes and horseradish crème fraîche

To me, there is nothing sweeter, richer, or more delicate than the taste of wild salmon when it is available during late spring and early summer. I choose not to serve farmed salmon at the restaurant, because I find its flavor inferior to its mighty wild cousin. Wild salmon is glorious almost any way, but I particularly like it served chilled and raw. The sweet, pickled flavor of green tomatoes works well with it here and the horseradish crème fraîche provides a creamy foil to the sharp tomatoes.

Serves 4

14 oz [400 g] firm, very fresh wild salmon fillet, skinned

A little mild-tasting extra virgin olive oil

A small handful frisée

A small handful mâche

Coarse sea salt and freshly ground black pepper

For the pickled tomato relish

14 Tbsp [200 ml] good quality red or white wine vinegar

¾ cup [150 g] superfine sugar

1 Tbsp fennel seeds

4 medium green tomatoes

For the horseradish crème fraîche

3 Tbsp freshly grated horseradish

¾ cup [180 ml] crème fraîche

Start by making the pickling liquor for the tomatoes. Put the wine vinegar, sugar, and fennel seeds into a saucepan over medium heat to dissolve the sugar. Bring to a boil, then lower the heat and simmer a couple of minutes. Remove from the heat and set aside to cool.

Meanwhile, chop the tomatoes into small, fairly even chunks and place in a bowl. Once the pickling liquor has cooled to warm, pour it over the tomatoes. Add a pinch of salt and stir well.

For the horseradish crème fraîche, put the grated horseradish in a bowl and stir in the crème fraîche. Taste and add a little salt if you think it is needed.

Using a very sharp, flexible knife, slice the raw salmon as finely as possible.

To assemble, arrange the salmon slices on plates, drizzle with a little olive oil, and season with salt. Pay particular attention to the seasoning—raw fish can be underwhelming if it is not seasoned sufficiently.

Scatter the frisée and mâche over the salmon. Spoon on the tomato relish sparingly, then finish with a little horseradish crème fraîche and a light sprinkling of pepper. Serve at once.

Crab with crème fraîche and roe

This combination of textures and flavors works beautifully and makes for a delicious yet simple appetizer. At the restaurant we serve it on individual plates, but you could just as well arrange it on one large plate in the center of the table for everyone to help themselves.

Preheat the oven to its lowest setting and warm the rye crackers gently on a sheet in the oven while you prepare the other ingredients.

Pick over the crab meat to remove any fragments of shell, then put in a bowl and season very sparingly with salt and just a little black pepper. Add about 1½ Tbsp olive oil and a few drops of lemon juice. Toss together very lightly but thoroughly with your fingertips.

In a separate bowl, dress the leaves with the remaining olive oil and lemon juice to taste. Season with salt and pepper and toss gently to coat.

Divide the crab meat among the plates and arrange the dressed leaves alongside. Spoon the crème fraîche on top of the crab and finish with the roe. Serve the warmed rye crackers on the side.

Serves 6

12¾ oz [360 g] freshly prepared white crab meat

2½ to 3 Tbsp mild-tasting extra virgin olive oil

Juice of ½ lemon, or to taste

A handful of mixed herb leaves, such as chervil, purslane, and mint, and/or arugula leaves

¾ cup [180 ml] crème fraîche

3½ oz [100 g] lumpfish roe

Sea salt and freshly ground black pepper

Rye crackers (see page 36), to serve

Spice-roasted quail with celery root and walnuts

Quail is one of my very favorite little birds. Deeply flavorful and deliciously plump, each one gives a few succulent mouthfuls and perfect little bones that are irresistible to gnaw on! This is an elegant and suave appetizer with complex and interesting flavors.

Preheat the oven to 400°F [200°C]. Place the quail in a bowl. Sprinkle over the spice mix and dried chili and season well with salt. Drizzle over 1 Tbsp olive oil and turn the quail to coat. Transfer the seasoned quail to a roasting tray.

Place the tomatoes in a small roasting tray, trickle over the wine vinegar and 2 Tbsp olive oil, and toss lightly. Season with a little salt.

Roast the quail on the top shelf of the oven, with the tomatoes on a shelf below, about 12 minutes until tender.

Meanwhile, peel the celery root and slice into fine rounds, then into matchsticks. Immediately drop into a bowl of cold water with a little lemon juice added to prevent discoloration. For the dressing, put the crème fraîche in a bowl with the mustard and a small pinch of salt and stir well to combine.

Once the quail are cooked, cover loosely with foil and rest in a warm place 10 minutes. Let the tomatoes cool slightly.

Meanwhile, dress the radicchio with lemon juice and olive oil, salt, and pepper to taste. Drain the celery root and toss in a separate bowl with the mustard dressing.

For the marjoram oil, pound the marjoram leaves with a pinch of salt, using a mortar and pestle, then gradually work in the olive oil—you will have a lovely thick sauce.

Arrange the salad leaves, tomatoes, and celery root on plates and sit the quail on top. Finish with a scattering of walnuts and a few spoonfuls of marjoram oil. Serve immediately.

Serves 4

4 quail

1 ½ Tbsp roasted spice mix (mixed coriander, cumin, fennel, and cardamom seeds, toasted and freshly ground)

1 dried red chili, crumbled

4 Tbsp extra virgin olive oil

About 12 baby plum tomatoes

½ Tbsp red wine vinegar

1 small celery root

Juice of ½ lemon, or to taste

1 small radicchio, leaves separated

12 to 16 shelled fresh walnuts

Sea salt and freshly ground black pepper

For the dressing

2 Tbsp crème fraîche

1 Tbsp Dijon mustard

For the marjoram oil

A bunch marjoram, leaves only

7 Tbsp [100 ml] extra virgin olive oil

Nettle risotto

*This is a wonderfully green, bright, and optimistic risotto, to be served
in the spring when nettles are growing everywhere. Be sure to wear gloves
when handling the nettles to avoid getting stung—it is worth noting that
the sting is in the stem and not in the leaves.*

Bring a large pot of water to a boil. Wash the nettles in a bowl of cool water. When the water comes to a rolling boil, plunge in the nettles and blanch 30 seconds. Drain the nettles and refresh them in cold water. Drain well and put the nettles into a food processor with about 1 Tbsp water. Purée until smooth.

Bring the stock to a boil in a pan, then turn down the heat to keep it at a simmer.

Melt the butter in a heavy-based wide pan. Add the onion and cook gently until soft and translucent, without coloring; this will take about 5 minutes. Tip in the rice and stir well to coat the grains in the butter and warm them. Now add the wine and let bubble until reduced right down.

Start to add the warm stock, a ladleful or 2 at a time, stirring gently but thoroughly as the stock is absorbed by the rice grains. Allow each addition of stock to be absorbed fully before adding the next ladleful. About 15 minutes into the cooking, add the nettle purée and stir well. Continue adding the stock until the rice is cooked through but still firm to the bite. The whole process will take about 18 minutes.

Take off the heat, put the lid on, and let the risotto rest 1 minute, then stir in the butter cubes and grated Parmesan. Season with salt and pepper to taste and serve at once.

Serves 6, or 4 for lunch

2 handfuls freshly picked nettles

2½ qt [2.5 L] chicken stock

¼ cup [50 g] unsalted butter

1 yellow onion, peeled and finely chopped

14 oz [400 g] arborio or carnaroli risotto rice

[130 ml] dry white wine

To finish

4½ Tbsp [60 g] unsalted butter, chilled and cut into cubes

1 cup [80 g] Parmesan, freshly grated

Sea salt and freshly ground black pepper

Chickpea soup with pancetta and sage

Full of satisfying flavors, this soup makes a lovely, warming wintry appetizer, although I more often have a larger bowl of it for lunch during the week with some good bread. Look for chickpeas that are creamy in color and consistency and not too wrinkly—indicating that they have been dried relatively recently. As they age, they tend to become shriveled, and darken.

Serves 6, or 4 for lunch

8¾ oz [250 g] dried chickpeas

1 bouquet garni (thyme, parsley, and bay)

1 garlic bulb, halved horizontally

1 ripe tomato, quartered

2 to 3 Tbsp extra virgin olive oil, plus extra to finish

6½ oz [180 g] pancetta, derinded and cut into strips

1 yellow onion, peeled and finely chopped

1 carrot, peeled and finely chopped

2 celery stalks, finely chopped

2 garlic cloves, peeled and crushed

6 sage sprigs

2 bay leaves

1 dried red chili

2 Tbsp tomato paste

Sea salt and freshly ground black pepper

Start the night before. Soak the chickpeas in plenty of cold water (ideally twice their volume) overnight.

The next day, drain the chickpeas, and put them in a large saucepan with the bouquet garni, halved garlic bulb, and tomato. Add 1 Tbsp olive oil (but no seasoning). Cover and bring to a boil, then turn the heat down to a simmer. Cook until the chickpeas are tender, topping up with water if necessary; this will take about 1½ hours. Take off the heat and set aside.

In a separate pan, heat a little olive oil over medium-low heat until warm, then add the pancetta, onion, carrot, and celery. Cook gently 10 minutes, until the vegetables are soft but not colored. Add the garlic, sage, and bay leaves, crumble in the chili, and cook a further 5 minutes. Now add the tomato paste and stir well to combine.

Drain the chickpeas, reserving the cooking liquor; discard the garlic and bouquet garni. Add a third of the chickpeas to the soup base. Tip the rest of them into a blender and add half of the reserved cooking liquor. Purée the chickpeas until smooth, adding a little more of the liquor if necessary—to get a good soupy consistency. Stir the chickpea purée into the soup and add more water if necessary—it should be thick and hearty but not cloying. Discard the sage and bay leaves. Season with plenty of salt and pepper.

Ladle into warm soup plates and add a generous drizzle of olive oil. Serve with warm crusty bread.

Potato and porcini soup

This is a simple soup—full of flavor and depth, but with a quiet elegance. The beautiful, mellow, musty flavor of porcini seeps into the flesh of the potatoes completely. Warming, calm, and comforting, it tastes of fall. Don't be alarmed by the quantity of olive oil—it is an integral part of the dish, enhancing the flavor and adding a luscious glossiness to the soup.

Serves 6, or 4 for lunch

1 Tbsp dried porcini

1 ¼ cups [300 ml] warm water

½ cup [120 ml] extra virgin olive oil

3 shallots, peeled and finely sliced

2 ¼ lb [1 kg] Roseval potatoes

3 tender rosemary sprigs, leaves only, finely chopped

3 garlic cloves, peeled and crushed

1 small dried red chili

¾ cup [60 g] Parmesan, freshly grated

Juice of ½ lemon

A bunch of curly parsley, leaves only, very finely chopped

Sea salt and freshly ground black pepper

Put the dried porcini in a bowl, pour on the warm water, and let soak 10 minutes to allow the porcini to soften and infuse their lovely, musty flavor into the water.

Put a large, wide, heavy-based pan over low heat and add 1 Tbsp olive oil. When it is warm, add the shallots. Cook over low heat, stirring from time to time, about 10 minutes to soften the shallots; don't allow them to color.

Slice the potatoes into ¼ in [5 mm] rounds (don't bother to peel them as the skin lends a delicious flavor to the soup).

Add the rosemary and garlic to the softened shallots, crumble over the chili, and stir well to combine.

Remove the soaked porcini from the water with a slotted spoon, reserving the water. Chop the mushrooms fairly roughly and add them to the pan along with the potatoes. Cook a couple of minutes, then pour over the reserved liquid, leaving any sediment in the bottom of the bowl. Stir well to combine and cook 5 minutes.

Add the rest of the olive oil, a large pinch of salt (as potatoes absorb and need a lot), and a little pepper. Put the lid on the pan and cook 10 minutes, stirring every now and then until the potatoes are just tender and starting to fall apart.

Add the Parmesan and lemon juice and sprinkle over the chopped parsley. Taste one final time and add what you feel is necessary—perhaps a little more pepper and a pinch or two of salt. Ladle the soup into warm bowls and serve.

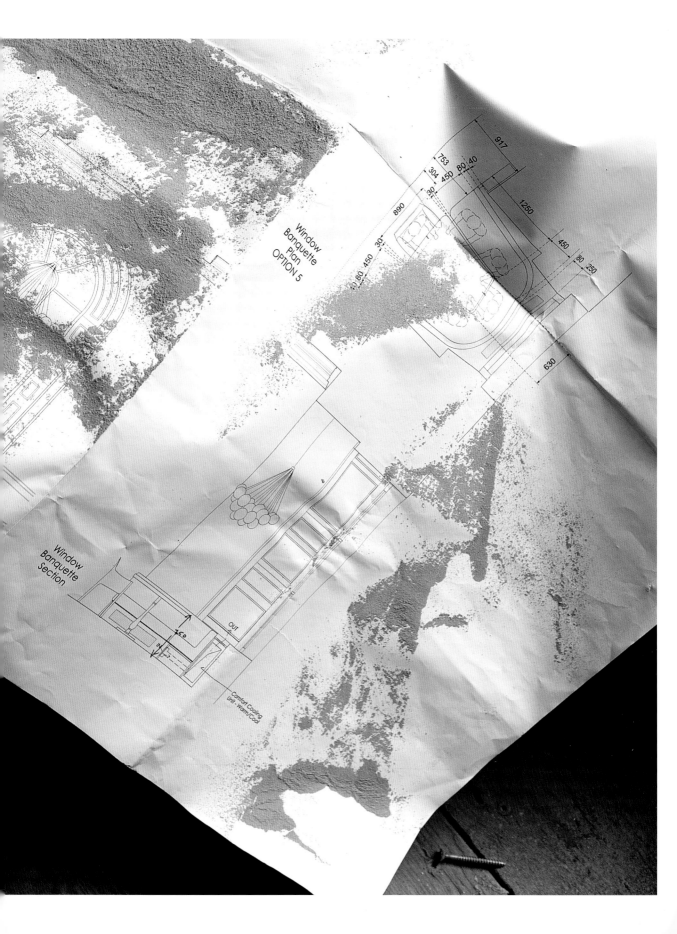

Window
Banquette
Plan
OPTION 5

Window
Banquette
Section

917
753
304 450 80 40
30
1250
890
30
40 80 450
450
80 250
630
OUT
150
IN
Comfort Cooling
Unit - Warm/Cool

The architect

Transforming Somerset House from a tax office to a beautiful restaurant was an ambitious project. Over the years the unloved space had been divided into smaller rooms. Sweeping, generous archways had been filled in and thick, cumbersome doors put in place. Fireplaces had been blocked up or moved to awkward places, and beautiful glass doorways had been turned into oddly proportioned windows. The impressive, tall ceiling wasn't conducive to a comfortable noise level for a restaurant and the cornicing that framed it was ornate and brutal.

Restoring the space to its former beauty and, at the same time, turning it into a functioning restaurant was a huge challenge. We needed an inspired architect with plenty of experience. Chef Ruth Rogers recommended Stuart Forbes, who had worked on the refit of the River Café after a fire. He visited us on site and I liked him immediately. He presented a scheme that was not only sympathetic to the space, but also provided us with a really strong back-of-house infrastructure—that would enable us to run the restaurant efficiently and allow us to grow in the future. Stuart's assistant Roberta actually took up residence in our office space above the restaurant and stayed for a large part of the project.

bread

Bread making is a craft and it does take a while to master, yet it is ultimately incredibly rewarding. As our bread making has evolved, we have found that we love the gently acidic flavor of loaves that are risen naturally, but dislike the distinct smell and taste that commercially produced yeast lends. Consequently, we now use a natural starter for all of our breads.

Making a starter is straightforward enough but it takes a little time to become really familiar with the process. The guideline is simple: you are always looking for a starter or "mother" that smells fresh and clean with a very gentle, pleasant acidity.

To make a starter

*If you're planning to make bread regularly, it is a good idea to keep
a wooden bowl especially for the purpose. After use, wipe the bowl gently
but essentially leave it unwashed. Each time you use the bowl, adding
water will wake up the residual microorganisms, the flour will nourish
them, and time will do the rest.*

1 ¼ cups [300 ml] tepid water,
plus extra to feed

About 2 ½ cups [300 g]
unbleached wholemeal flour,
plus extra to feed

Pour the water into a large wooden bowl. Gradually whisk
in flour until the mixture is the texture of loose yogurt. Leave,
uncovered, overnight in a fairly warm, draught-free room
(ideally at around 80°F [27°C]).

In the morning the mixture should be alive and slightly
frothy. If it isn't frothy, feed it with a little more water and
flour every day until it is.

Your starter should be ready to use in 7 to 10 days. It should
smell clean and fresh and mildly acidic. If it doesn't smell
fresh or it tastes very acidic, you will have to start again.

Sourdough

*In the spring of 2013 we headed to Darina Allen's Ballymaloe Cookery
School in Ireland for a two-day workshop with Chad Robertson from
Tartine Bakery in San Francisco. Chad is perhaps the most influential
baker in the world today. It was an inspiring experience.
He is so connected with his ingredients, so gentle with his hands,
and he works in a very restrained way—hardly kneading the
bread at all. We learned so much from him.*

*Inspired by Chad's porridge bread, this is my favorite bread recipe—
it has a wonderful texture—creamy, yet chewy with lots of unrefined
crunchy seeds in it. Beautiful just as it is, I also love it toasted and
eaten with butter.*

*All the ingredients need to be very fresh, especially the nuts, otherwise
the final result will take on a slightly rancid flavor. The bread should
have a vibrant, nutty, and clean flavor.*

Makes 2 loaves

For the leaven (starter dough)

1 Tbsp starter (see page 29)

14 Tbsp [200 ml] warm water (at 77°F [25°C])

⅞ cup [100 g] strong white bread flour

⅞ cup [100 g] unrefined wholemeal bread flour

For the porridge mixture

¼ cup [50 g] unprocessed barley

¼ cup [50 g] unprocessed brown rice

1¼ cups [100 g] steel-cut oats

⅔ cup [50 g] rolled oats

⅜ cup [50 g] linseeds

⅜ cup [50 g] sunflower seeds

½ cup [50 g] Brazil nuts, roughly chopped

A good pinch of salt

For the bread

5¼ oz [150 g] leaven (starter dough)

3⅛ cups [750 ml] water

5½ tsp salt

4⅛ cups [500 g] strong white bread flour, plus extra to dust

4⅛ cups [500 g] unrefined wholemeal bread flour

4½ Tbsp [70 g] wheatgerm

1⅛ lb [500 g] cooked oat porridge (see above)

Rice flour, to dust

Rolled oats, for coating

For the leaven, the night before making the bread, put the 1 Tbsp starter into a container. Feed it with the warm water and the white and wholemeal flour. Mix together with your hands until you have a loose dough. Cover with a dish towel and leave in a cool room overnight (ideally at 64°F [18°C]).

The following morning, to test your leaven, place a spoonful in a bowl of tepid water (at 98°F [37°C]). If the leaven floats, it is ready to use; if it sinks, it is not and needs a little more time to ferment and ripen. At this stage you can speed up the process slightly by putting it in a warmer spot and checking it every half hour. Once the leaven is ready, you can make your bread.

For the porridge mixture, place all the grains, seeds, and nuts in a bowl and pour on enough water to just cover them. Cover the bowl with plastic wrap and leave to soak in the refrigerator 2 hours.

Transfer the soaked grain mixture to a saucepan and add twice their volume of water and a good pinch of salt. Cook, stirring frequently, over medium-low heat 5 minutes until the grains are just tender and the water is absorbed. Set aside to cool—as the mixture cools it will firm up and form a slight skin on the surface.

To make the bread, put the leaven in a bowl with the water and salt. Combine the flours and wheatgerm and pile into a mound on a clean work surface. Make a hollow in the center and pour in the leaven liquid, all at once, slowly and carefully. Gently draw handfuls of flour from the outside into the center and mix together with your hands to combine all the wet and dry ingredients. Continue until you have a thick, cohesive dough.

Now start kneading. The mixture will be very loose at this stage—it may seem too runny, but resist any temptation to add more flour. Simply keep kneading to develop the gluten and the dough will start to develop and come together as it should. This will take about 30 minutes. (To save time and effort, you can knead it in a mixer instead, in which case it will take about 10 minutes.) At the end of this time the dough should still be soft and sticky.

Dust the dough with a little flour, cover with a clean dish towel, and leave to rest on the work surface a couple of hours. The cloth will have stuck to the sticky risen dough. To release it, spray with water using a spray bottle and leave for a couple of minutes, then peel off the cloth. It should come away cleanly. Fold the cooked oat porridge through the dough, kneading very gently once or twice.

Divide the dough in half and shape each piece into a ball with a smooth, taut surface. Line two proving baskets with clean, dry cloths and dust generously with a mixture of rice and wheat flour. Coat the surface of the dough with rolled oats by rolling the smooth side in the oats. Now upturn the loaves into the cloth-lined proving baskets, so they are coated side down. Cover loosely with a clean, dry cloth and leave to prove in the refrigerator overnight.

Preheat the oven to 425°F [220°C]. Put 2 cast-iron 9½ in [24 cm] round bread pots with lids in the oven to get really hot. Flour the pots generously and then carefully tip the risen dough into them, so the oat-coated surface is uppermost. Put the lids on and bake 40 minutes, removing the lids from the pots 10 minutes before the end of cooking to allow the crust to color to a deep golden brown. (If your oven is not big enough you may have to cook the bread in 2 batches.) If the crust appears to be overdarkening, lower the oven temperature slightly.

To check that the loaves are ready, remove them from the pots and tap the base firmly with your knuckles; the bread should sound hollow.

Transfer the loaves to a wire rack to cool completely and allow the crumb to open and the crust to harden before slicing and eating.

Rye bread

I first paid a visit to Shipton Mill in Gloucestershire, England a couple of years ago, to learn more about the flours we were using in our breads. John, Shipton's owner, and his team, taught us a lot about flours and bread making and in return we gave them cooking tips. Our collaboration culminated in a Harvest Festival that we cooked together in the fall of 2013. This seeded rye is based on a recipe given to us by Clive, head baker at Shipton Mill. Wonderfully sticky and laden with seeds, it has a closed crumb and good crust. It's so good that I usually double up the quantities at home and make two loaves.

Makes 1 loaf

2 tsp sesame seeds

2 Tbsp poppy seeds

2 Tbsp linseeds

2 Tbsp pumpkin seeds

2 Tbsp sunflower seeds

2½ cups [300 g] light rye flour (at 77 to 82°F [25 to 28°C]), plus extra to dust

10½ oz [300 g] starter (see page 29)

1 ⅞ tsp salt

9½ Tbsp [140 ml] warm water (at 77 to 82°F [25 to 28°C])

Rice flour, to dust

Coarse semolina, to dust (optional)

Put all the seeds in a bowl, pour on enough water (at room temperature) to cover, and leave to soak overnight.

The following day, check the temperature of your ingredients with a thermometer: 77 to 82°F [25 to 28°C] is the optimum level of warmth for your yeast to grow. Put the flour, starter, and salt in a bowl. Drain off any excess water from the soaked seeds, then add them to the flour mixture. Add the water and mix well with your hands to form a smooth dough. Leave to rest 30 minutes.

Turn the dough out onto a lightly floured surface and knead lightly, then cover loosely and leave to rise 1 hour.

Flour a proving basket very generously with a mixture of rye flour and rice flour. Place the dough in the basket and cover loosely with a floured cloth. Leave to prove in a warm, draught-free place for 1½ hours.

Preheat your oven to 425°F [220°C]. When the oven is really hot, generously flour a flat baking sheet with coarse semolina or rice flour (this will stop the bread from sticking) and place the sheet in the oven to heat up. Once the sheet is hot, invert your risen dough onto it and bake in the oven 40 minutes.

This bread tastes even better the day after it is made and will keep well 3 to 4 days; the flavor matures as the bread ages.

Rye crackers

We make these crackers every day—they have a wonderful rye flavor and delicious crunch. We serve them on our cheese plate, or occasionally break them into little shards and toss them through salads. Don't be deceived by their slim proportions—they are strong enough to take all manner of toppings. Try them with a spoonful of the freshest ricotta and a drizzle of honey. At the restaurant, we add a little of our rye bread starter to the dough but I make them at home successfully without any starter at all.

Put the rye flour, salt, and honey in a large bowl and make a well in the middle. Pour in the water and mix together, using your hands, to a homogeneous dough. Wrap in plastic wrap and chill in the refrigerator for 1 hour.

Preheat the oven to 350°F [180°C]. Take the dough from the refrigerator. On a lightly floured surface, roll it out to a very thin sheet and cut into long triangles or rectangles. Put on a baking sheet.

Bake on the middle shelf of the oven 8 to 12 minutes until crisp and golden brown. Transfer to a wire rack to cool.

Makes 20 to 25

2⅛ cups [250 g] organic wholegrain rye flour, plus extra to dust

½ tsp sea salt

1½ tsp honey

9½ Tbsp [140 ml] water

dairy

Butter

I first came across butter making a decade ago while I was attending a Slow Food Harvest Festival at Darina Allen's Ballymaloe Cookery School in Ireland. I had gone to teach there and stayed on to help at the Harvest Festival. After several hours working, I was searching for a place to hide and rest, so I slipped into one of the cookery rooms. A class on butter making was in progress and I was struck by the simplicity of the process, and drawn in by its romanticism. It was the first time I had really thought about butter, other than how it tasted and which brand I preferred. It was an enlightening moment when I realized that butter was originally made as a way of preserving dairy outside of the milking season. I've always prided myself on knowing exactly what was in season—and when—but never in regards to dairy produce. It gave me pause for thought. When I returned home, I tried making butter for myself.

It has only been in the last couple of years that I have made butter on a continual basis and started experimenting with different creams to see which I prefer and how they react. I've tried butter beaten until it is hard; whipped so gently that it still contains a little buttermilk; salted and unsalted; washed and unwashed; flavored with caraway and bone marrow. All are delicious in their own way but this recipe, which is generously salted with really good quality salt, is the one that complements the bread we make better than any other.

It is important to use really good quality cream. I prefer unpasteurized cream, mainly for reasons of taste but also because I believe that it is better for you. I also like to culture the cream, which improves the flavor and gives it the depth and character that I am looking for. You can also wash the butter if you prefer, which is a process of rinsing the butter under cool running water to extract any excess buttermilk that is still contained within. This will give the butter a longer shelf life but I'm happy leaving it in—we make butter daily so it's not an issue for us.

Makes just over 1 cup [250 g]

2½ cups [600 ml] organic, unpasteurized cream

2 Tbsp organic, unpasteurized plain yogurt

1 tsp good quality salt (I use pink Himalayan salt)

A day ahead of making the butter, put the cream into a bowl. Add the yogurt and stir well to combine. Put a clean cloth over the top of the bowl and let it stand in a warm place, 70°F [21°C] ideally, 8 to 12 minutes.

The cream is ready when it has thickened slightly and has a gentle foam on its surface. It will also have a mildly acidic smell. Leave the cream in the refrigerator 1 hour to chill.

Transfer the cultured cream to the bowl of an electric mixer. Put a clean cloth over the top of the mixer (this will prevent the buttermilk splashing out over the top) and set the whisk speed to medium-high. The mixture will soon turn to thickly whipped cream. As you continue to mix, it will become grainy, then form a mass of butter as the buttermilk quickly separates out. As soon as the buttermilk begins to split from the butter, stop the machine. Remove the butter that has formed with clean hands.

Don't discard the buttermilk. It has all kinds of uses, such as scones, desserts (see page 159), and salad dressings (see page 57) and will keep a few days in the refrigerator until you are ready to use it.

At this stage, you can rinse the butter under cold running water, if you wish. Now add the salt and work it in with your fingers until evenly incorporated.

Shape the butter with your hands and wrap in parchment paper. Put in the refrigerator until ready to use; it will keep well a couple of days.

Yogurt

I initially started making yogurt while the restaurant was being painstakingly built. I had the opportunity to attempt so many things in the kitchen that I'd always wanted to do but never found the time for. I started with the fundamentals: bread, butter, yogurt; later moving on to pickling and preserving. It was these time-honored, almost forgotten, skills that really intrigued me. To me, they are the very staff of life.

I have always loved yogurt. Cool, sharp, and creamy, I adore its purity of flavor, but also like to use it as a base for sauces, laced with vibrant fresh herbs, freshly chopped garlic or chili, turmeric, honey, and spices. It makes for a delicious marinade, dressing, or topping.

Yogurt is easy and satisfying to make. There are just a couple of important factors to bear in mind. First, the live yogurt you add must have a taste that you particularly like, as it will ultimately influence the flavor of the yogurt that you are making. Second, in order to nourish and promote the healthy bacteria to be found in yogurt, the milk must be at the correct temperature, so a cook's thermometer is useful.

If you prefer a thicker, denser yogurt—in the style of labne—hang your yogurt in clean muslin over a bowl overnight.

Makes about 2 qt [2 L]

2⅓ qt [2.25 L] organic whole milk

1¼ cups [300 ml] heavy cream

1⅛ cups [250 ml] fresh live yogurt

Pour the milk into a large, heavy-based stainless steel pan and bring to a boil. Turn the heat down and simmer very gently, stirring now and then until it is has reduced by a third. Take off the heat, pour into a bowl, and stir in the cream. Let cool.

Once the mixture has cooled to tepid (98°F [37°C]), add the yogurt and stir to combine. Cover the bowl with plastic wrap, then wrap completely in a clean cloth (to exclude light) and keep in a warm place (at about 104°F [40°C]) overnight.

The following morning, transfer to the refrigerator. The yogurt will keep around 5 days.

Ricotta

I love ricotta and use it a lot in cooking, to fill ravioli or spoon over warm vegetables, for example. I started making it when I was experimenting with young curd cheeses. Although it is often referred to as a cheese, ricotta is actually a by-product of cheese making. The whey that is drained off from the cheese curds is reheated to make ricotta—hence the name, which translates as "recooked."

My recipe for ricotta, however, is made by gently heating whole milk, then adding a little vinegar to encourage little curds to form. I've tried using buttermilk and lemon juice, but found vinegar gives better results. The quantity of vinegar is all-important: too little and the curds won't form properly; too much and the end result will taste unpleasantly acidic. Because this recipe is so simple, it is essential to use fine quality ingredients. The best ricotta I have made used raw, unpasteurized milk, though this is hard to come by. Ricotta tends to spoil easily, so it needs to be used within a day or so of making.

Pour the milk into a large nonreactive pan, add the salt, and put over medium heat. Heat the milk slowly, stirring from time to time. When it is almost coming to a boil, i.e. when steam and small bubbles begin to appear on the surface, check the temperature with a thermometer; it should register between 179 and 185°F [82 and 85°C]. Remove from the heat, add the vinegar, and stir gently. You will see curds starting to form. Continue to stir 1 minute or so. Cover with a clean cloth and allow the mixture to sit a couple of hours.

Once the ricotta has rested, line a colander with a large piece of dampened muslin and put over a larger bowl or pan. Spoon the ricotta into the colander and allow to drain an hour or so. To test whether the cheese is ready, gently lift the muslin up by the corners and twist lightly—the liquid should be slightly milky in color. The ricotta is now ready. Transfer to a container, seal, and store in the refrigerator until ready to use; it is best eaten within a day or two.

Makes about 2 cups [500 g]

2⅓ qt [2.25 L] organic whole milk

¼ tsp sea salt

3 Tbsp [40 ml] good quality distilled white vinegar

The name

The name was one of the hardest decisions. I wanted it to be happy and energetic, short and easy to pronounce and spell. Ideally, it would convey a sense of optimism and make you smile. I soon learned that settling on a name is not an easy thing to do. It's not something that you can change if you become tired or bored of it. Like naming a child, it remains for life. "Somerset" sounded noble and elegant, but it didn't feel quite right. Numerous other ideas were considered and rejected, and for nearly five months the project chugged along without a name.

"Spring" came to me slowly. When it was first suggested, it didn't particularly stand out for me, but the more I thought about it the more appropriate it seemed. The fact that it starts with an "S" was appealing, because I love the shape. There is something about its deep, generous lower curve that reminds me of a treble clef and I've always thought about food musically. Dishes are compositions to me, their individual flavors musical notes, that when brought together, create something beautiful, whole, and complete. With just five letters, it was short and easy to spell too. And there was a nod to the seasons, which is what inspires and stimulates my cooking. Finally, and most importantly, the word itself suggests new beginnings and exudes energy and optimism. Spring it became.

Once the name was in place, the project began to feel much more real. We had a site and a name. Now we just had to find a way of making the project work . . .

salads

Little gem, candied walnuts, and Caesar dressing

*There is nothing better than a really good Caesar salad. At its finest, it's
a simple, beautiful combination of ingredients, laced and stitched together
by an unctuous dressing. The dressing is easy enough to get right but so
often very disappointing—the trick is to use the best possible ingredients.
I like to serve this salad with bruschetta, placed on the middle of the table,
for everyone to mop up all the wonderful flavors.*

First prepare the candied walnuts. Preheat the oven to 400°F [200°C]. Lay the walnut halves on a baking sheet and toast on the middle shelf of the oven 2 minutes, being careful that they don't burn. Remove from the oven and set aside.

Tip the sugar into a small heavy-based pan, put over medium heat, and stir with a wooden spoon until the sugar melts and begins to color. Cook 1 minute or so, until the sugar syrup is a warm amber color. Add the nuts and stir to coat the nuts in the syrup. Remove from the heat and spread out on a sheet lined with baking parchment to cool. Sprinkle with salt and set aside until ready to use.

For the dressing, put the garlic, mustard powder, anchovies, egg yolk, lemon juice, and Parmesan into a food processor and blitz for a few seconds to combine, then with the motor running, slowly drizzle in the olive oil through the funnel. (It's important that you do this as slowly as possible to ensure that the dressing doesn't curdle.) Transfer to a bowl and stir in the crème fraîche. Thin to a pouring consistency with a little warm water.

Separate the lettuce leaves, leaving them whole. Wash and pat dry, then arrange attractively in individual bowls or on a large platter. Spoon over the dressing, then shave some Parmesan over the salad. Scatter over the candied nuts and finish with the chopped parsley and chives. Serve at once.

Serves 4 to 6

2 heads of little gem lettuce

A small piece Parmesan

A small bunch flat-leaf parsley, leaves only, finely chopped

A small bunch chives, very finely chopped

For the Caesar dressing

2 garlic cloves, peeled and roughly chopped

1½ tsp mustard powder

3 good quality anchovies (my favorite is Ortiz)

1 organic free-range egg yolk

Juice of 1 lemon

2 Tbsp freshly grated Parmesan

14 Tbsp [200 ml] mild-tasting extra virgin olive oil

2 Tbsp crème fraîche

A splash of warm water

For the candied walnuts

1⅓ cups [150 g] shelled walnuts

½ cup [100 g] granulated sugar

A good pinch sea salt

Salad of beets, tomatoes, goat's curd, and radicchio

This is really just an excuse to put as many beautiful summer vegetables on a plate as possible. The sweet, earthy taste of beets works well with baby fava beans and ripe tomatoes, while the radicchio lends a contrasting slightly bitter note and the goat's curd underpins the lightness. Chioggia beets, with its candy-striped flesh, is a lovely inclusion if you have it. Serve this salad as an appetizer, or with a plate of cured meats and some freshly baked sourdough for a light lunch.

Serves 4

12 small beets (ideally a mix of ruby, yellow, and Chioggia varieties)

2 Tbsp red wine vinegar

About 3½ Tbsp [50 ml] extra virgin olive oil

7 oz [200 g] baby fava beans, freshly podded

About 8 large radicchio leaves

About 8 little gem lettuce leaves

Juice of ½ lemon

4 to 6 ripe tomatoes, depending on size (ideally a heritage variety)

7 oz [200 g] goat's curd or young goat's cheese

2 Tbsp good quality black olives, pitted (optional)

Small handful basil leaves

Sea salt and freshly ground black pepper

For the basil oil

A bunch of basil, leaves only

7 Tbsp [100 ml] extra virgin olive oil

Scrub the beets well under cool running water, then put in a saucepan and pour on enough water to cover. Add a good pinch of salt and bring to a boil over medium heat. Lower the heat slightly and cook about 35 minutes until just tender when pierced with a sharp knife.

Once cooked, drain the beets and put in a bowl. Add the wine vinegar and about 2 Tbsp of the olive oil, season with salt and pepper, and toss gently to coat the beets in the dressing. Set aside to macerate and cool.

Blanch the fava beans in boiling water 1 minute, then drain and refresh in cold water; drain well.

Put the radicchio and lettuce leaves in another bowl. Dress with the lemon juice, remaining olive oil, and some salt and pepper, and toss lightly using your hands. Slice the tomatoes or halve them if small.

For the basil oil, pound the basil leaves using a mortar and pestle to bruise and break up, then gradually work in the olive oil—you will have a lovely thick sauce.

To assemble, arrange the salad leaves on serving plates with the beets and tomatoes. Add the goat's curd and scatter over the fava beans and the olives, if using. Spoon on the basil oil and finish with the basil leaves. Serve at once.

Raw cabbage, fennel, and pecorino salad

This simple salad is perfect for the early weeks of fall when the sun is still slightly warm and the season's beautiful ingredients are beginning to trickle in. I like to use the ruffley Savoy cabbage because I love its texture and sweet, mild taste—look for tender, young cabbages, with vibrant leaves. This salad works best if dressed an hour or so before serving. It's lovely as an appetizer, with a few slices of the finest Parma ham alongside.

Wash the cabbage under cool running water, separating the leaves as you do so by snapping them off at the base. Pat each leaf dry, using a clean dish towel, then slice into fine ribbons and put in a bowl.

Remove the fibrous outer layer of the fennel, and then slice the bulb in half lengthwise. Cut each half into very fine slices and add them to the cabbage ribbons in the bowl.

Add the pecorino slices and chopped parsley, then season the salad with salt and plenty of pepper. Drizzle over the olive oil and wine vinegar and toss really well to combine.

Leave the salad to sit 1 hour or so, to allow the vinegar to soften and wilt the leaves slightly, before serving.

Serves 6

1 Savoy cabbage

1 fennel bulb

5¼ oz [150 g] pecorino, finely sliced

A small bunch flat-leaf parsley, leaves only, finely chopped

½ cup [120 ml] extra virgin olive oil

3 tsp good quality red wine vinegar

Sea salt and freshly ground pepper

Slaw with pears, toasted hazelnuts, and buttermilk dressing

There is nothing quite like a really good coleslaw. It makes for an excellent side, especially with grilled meats or rich slow-cooked dishes, such as shoulder of pork. It's easy to prepare and, unlike most salads, really benefits from being dressed a couple of hours in advance, to allow time for the flavors to develop and mellow. You can add and subtract ingredients as you like, but I think this salad needs both a nutty crunch and a little fruity sweetness to make it really interesting. The dressing, which includes buttermilk and cider vinegar, gives it a creamy, yet gutsy, finish.

Serves 6

1 cup [120 g] shelled and skinned hazelnuts

¼ red cabbage, cored

¼ white cabbage, cored

1 fennel bulb, peeled

3 firm ripe pears

A bunch flat-leaf parsley, leaves only

Sea salt and freshly ground black pepper

For the dressing

1 organic free-range egg yolk

½ Tbsp Dijon mustard

1 ½ tsp honey

1 Tbsp good quality cider vinegar

¾ cup [180 ml] mild-tasting extra virgin olive oil

2 Tbsp buttermilk

Preheat the oven to 350°F [180°C]. Spread the hazelnuts out on a baking sheet and toast them on the middle shelf of the oven 4 to 5 minutes. Remove from the oven and let cool, then chop roughly.

Finely slice both the red and white cabbage into thin ribbons and put in a bowl. Remove the tough, fibrous outer layer from the fennel, cut the bulb in half lengthwise, and then slice very finely. Add to the cabbage.

Halve the pears, remove the core, and then slice finely. Add to the bowl of cabbage and fennel, toss lightly, and season well with salt and plenty of pepper. Set aside while you make the dressing.

Put the egg yolk, mustard, honey, and vinegar into a small bowl. Season with a little salt and pepper and stir vigorously to combine. Now whisk in the olive oil slowly, almost drip by drip to begin with, increasing the flow slightly once the dressing begins to homogenize. Continue until all the oil is incorporated. Stir in the buttermilk, then taste and adjust the seasoning as necessary.

Pour the dressing over the salad and mix together gently but thoroughly using your fingertips. Set aside in a cool place 1 or 2 hours before serving.

Spinach, wild herbs, and goat's curd

I was first introduced to foraging a decade ago by Miles Irving when he arrived at Petersham Nurseries with the most beautiful wild herbs. A few years later, I spent a fascinating day with him in the Hampshire countryside foraging for edible plants. I remember eating bullrush that day—clean and crunchy, a little like a water chestnut—and pineapple weed, which smells more like pineapple than the fruit itself. One word of caution: if you do decide to forage, ensure that the ground from which you are picking is clean, use a guide book until you feel confident, and wash the herbs really well under gently flowing water before using.

Wash the spinach really well under cold running water and shake gently to remove the excess water. Put a pan, large enough to hold the spinach comfortably, over low heat and add the spinach with just the water clinging to the leaves after washing. Cook until the leaves have just wilted, tossing them once or twice to ensure they heat evenly.

Immediately remove from the heat and drain the spinach in a colander, then set aside until cool enough to handle. Squeeze out the excess water using your hands—it is important to remove as much water from the spinach as possible, otherwise the dressing on the leaves will be diluted and taste watery.

Put the spinach in a bowl and add half the lemon juice and a quarter of the olive oil. Season with salt and pepper.

Halve, stone, and chop the olives fairly finely. Put in a bowl and pour over the rest of the olive oil. Add the chopped parsley and lemon zest and stir well to combine.

Gently wash and pat dry the foraged herbs. Add them to the spinach and toss together using your fingertips. Taste and adjust the seasoning, adding a little more lemon juice if you think it is needed.

Put a generous spoonful of goat's curd on each serving plate and pile the spinach and herbs alongside. Spoon over the olive dressing and serve at once. This salad really calls for some warm bread on the side.

Serves 4

7 oz [200 g] spinach leaves

Finely grated zest and juice of ½ lemon

7 Tbsp [100 ml] extra virgin olive oil

20 black olives

4 flat-leaf parsley sprigs, finely chopped

A handful foraged herbs (such as wood sorrel, pennywort, pineapple weed, and dandelion)

7¾ oz [220 g] young fresh goat's curd

Sea salt and freshly ground black pepper

Spelt, anchovies, and mint

*This salad originally came about as a way of using up leftover grain.
At least once a week at home I will put a large pot of spelt on to cook when
I come home from work. It's quick, easy, warm, and comforting. We eat
it simply dressed with some good oil and a splash of wine vinegar,
sometimes with a fried egg on top.*

Put the spelt in a colander and rinse well under cool, running water, stopping when the water runs clear. Tip the spelt into a heavy-based saucepan and add enough cold water to cover by ¾ to 1 in [2 to 3 cm]. Bring to a boil over medium heat, then turn down the heat slightly. Cook until the spelt is tender but still firm to the bite—this will take about 25 to 35 minutes.

Drain the spelt and put in a bowl. While it is still warm, add the olive oil, wine vinegar, and a good pinch of salt. Toss together well to combine and set aside to cool.

While the spelt is cooling, quarter the cucumbers lengthwise, then chop them into ⅜ in [1 cm] pieces. Halve the tomatoes and tear the anchovies in half.

Once the spelt is cooled, add the cucumbers, tomatoes, anchovies, and lemon zest. Toss lightly together, then add the herbs and toss gently again. Squeeze over the lemon juice, taste for seasoning, and give the salad one final toss. Arrange prettily in a salad bowl or divide among plates.

Serves 4

7 oz [200 g] spelt

7 Tbsp [100 ml] extra virgin olive oil

2 Tbsp red wine vinegar

2 firm, ripe, small cucumbers

20 ripe little tomatoes, such as datterini, San Marzano, or organic cherry tomatoes

8 good quality anchovies (such as Ortiz)

Finely grated zest of 1 lemon and juice of ½ lemon

A large handful mint leaves, whole or roughly torn

A small bunch flat-leaf parsley, leaves only, chopped

A large handful basil leaves, whole or roughly torn

Sea salt and freshly ground black pepper

Octopus salad with potatoes, capers, and olives

*Octopus—cooked slowly until it is meltingly tender—is wonderful to eat
and its long, languid, purple-colored tentacles have a striking appearance
on the plate. Scattered with capers and olives, and accompanied by nutty
young potatoes and cima di rapa, it tastes perfect at room temperature. As
a rule, I am averse to the use of frozen food, but this cephalopod is an
exception—octopus that has been frozen first gives a much more tender
end result. (Illustrated on previous page.)*

Preheat the oven to 350°F [180°C]. Rinse the octopus well
under cold running water. Now prize out its beak at the
center of its head (it will pop out easily). Bring a large pot of
water to a boil. Plunge the octopus into the boiling water,
bring back to a boil, then lift the octopus out of the water
and place directly in a large roasting tin.

Pour on the wine and olive oil, and add about 4½ cups [1 L]
water to the roasting tin. Scatter the thyme sprigs, parsley
stalks, bay leaves, and peppercorns over the octopus. Cover
the tin securely with foil and cook on the middle shelf of the
oven 1½ hours. Remove from the oven and set aside to cool.

While the octopus is cooling, prepare the rest of the salad.
Put the potatoes in a pan, cover with cold water, add a large
pinch of salt, and cook over medium heat until tender when
pierced with a small, sharp knife. Drain the potatoes, cut
into quarters, and dress with a little extra virgin oil and
lemon juice while still warm. Set aside.

Bring a pan of water to a boil and salt it well. Add the cima
di rapa leaves and cook 2 minutes (just 1 minute for spinach).
Drain and toss through the potatoes.

For the dressing, put the olives and capers into a bowl, add
the parsley, lemon juice to taste, some salt and pepper, and
a generous glug of extra virgin olive oil. Stir to combine.

To serve, drain the octopus, cut into manageable pieces, and
divide among plates. Pile the potatoes and cima alongside
and spoon over the dressing. Serve with lemon wedges.

Serves 6 to 8

For the octopus

1 octopus (about 4½ lb
[2 kg]), frozen and fully
defrosted

1½ cups [350 ml] dry
white wine

7 Tbsp [100 ml] olive oil

A small bunch thyme sprigs

A small bunch flat-leaf parsley,
stalks and leaves separated

2 bay leaves

15 black peppercorns

For the salad

1½ lb [700 g] little potatoes
(ideally Roseval or Ratte)

Extra virgin olive oil, for
dressing

Juice of 1 lemon, or to taste

A bunch of cima di rapa,
trimmed and well rinsed
(or you could use spinach)

20 black olives

1½ Tbsp capers, well rinsed

A small bunch flat-leaf parsley,
leaves only, chopped

Sea salt and freshly ground
black pepper

Lemon wedges, to serve

Crab salad with chili, squash, curry leaves, and lime

I always say, whenever asked, that some sort of salad would have to be my last meal on earth—I'm not sure exactly which salad I'd choose, but this one would be a contender. The flavors and textures harmonize perfectly. One reason why I love salads is because food eaten at room temperature tastes particularly good. Flavors can really be appreciated and enjoyed when neither piping hot or really cold, and to this end you should never serve the ingredients straight from the refrigerator.

Serves 4

8¾ oz [250 g] butternut squash

Pinch of salt

8¾ oz [250 g] white crab meat

1 red chili, halved lengthwise, seeded, and finely chopped

8 fresh curry leaves

For the dressing

1 Tbsp finely chopped fresh ginger

½ tsp palm sugar

Juice of 1 lime

2 tsp fish sauce

Peel the butternut squash, discarding any seeds, then chop into small cubes. Put in a saucepan and add enough cold water to just cover, plus a pinch of salt. Bring to a boil, turn the heat down to a simmer. Cook until the squash is tender when pierced with a small, sharp knife; about 15 to 20 minutes. Drain and set aside to cool.

Now make the dressing. Using a mortar and pestle, gently pound the ginger and palm sugar to a smooth paste, then stir in the lime juice and fish sauce.

Put the crab, chili, and cooked squash in a bowl. Using a sharp knife, finely slice the curry leaves and add them to the salad. Spoon over the dressing and toss together lightly with your fingers. Divide the salad among individual plates and serve at once.

Roast chicken, tarragon, and gorgonzola salad

In some ways this salad seems almost like a cliché, but I love it. I've always been enamoured with the Cobb salad—a similarly glorious and colorful combination that includes chicken, bacon and blue cheese. As for all these salads, the ingredients need to be of really good quality, and care and attention must be paid at every stage of both the cooking and assembly. Look to balance the flavors, tasting and adjusting as necessary, to ensure you achieve a perfect harmony.

Serves 4 to 6

1 organic free-range chicken, about 3 lb [1.4 kg]

1 lemon, halved

A small bunch thyme

2 bay leaves

3 garlic cloves, halved

Olive oil, to drizzle

Sea salt and freshly ground black pepper

For the salad

3 Tbsp homemade mayonnaise

A small bunch thyme, leaves only

Finely grated zest and juice of 1 lemon

8 slices of pancetta

2 inner celery stalks (the paler stalks around the heart)

3 ripe tomatoes (heritage or San Marzano)

1 ripe avocado

20 freshly shelled walnuts, lightly toasted and roughly chopped

3½ oz [100 g] gorgonzola (or other blue cheese of your choice)

3 Tbsp olive oil

1 radicchio, finely shredded

A handful arugula leaves

1 Tbsp each chopped chives, tarragon, basil, and flat-leaf parsley

Preheat the oven to 400°F [200°C]. Put a lemon half into the chicken cavity with the thyme, bay leaves, and garlic. Squeeze the juice from the other lemon half over the chicken, then drizzle with olive oil. Season generously with salt and pepper, inside and out.

Put the chicken in a roasting tray and roast 15 minutes, then lower the setting to 350°F [180°C] and roast a further 45 minutes or until cooked through. To test, pierce the thickest part of the thigh with a skewer—the juices should run clear. Transfer to a board to cool.

Take the meat off the chicken and pull it apart by hand into large bite-size pieces. Put the chicken in a bowl and add the mayonnaise, thyme leaves, and a little lemon juice. Toss together gently, using your fingertips.

Preheat the grill to high and grill the pancetta until just crisp, then chop roughly.

Cut the celery and tomatoes into ⅜ in [1 cm] pieces. Halve, stone, and peel the avocado, then cut into ⅜ in [1 cm] cubes.

Place the celery, tomatoes, avocado, toasted walnuts, and pancetta in a bowl and crumble in the gorgonzola. Dress with lemon juice and 2 Tbsp olive oil, and season with a little salt and pepper.

Put the radicchio in a bowl and dress separately with the remainder of the olive oil and lemon juice. Add the arugula and herbs and toss lightly together.

To serve, layer the salad ingredients, starting with the shredded radicchio, arugula, and herbs, followed by the tomatoes, pancetta, and gorgonzola mix, then the chicken. Repeat the layers once or twice, then serve, sprinkled with a little lemon zest.

pasta

Making and shaping fresh pasta

I have found that the simplest and best fresh pasta is made with nothing more than flour, good quality very fresh eggs, and a little salt. You can make it in a food processor or by hand. As we make it in fairly large quantities in the restaurant, we use a food processor; at home I enjoy making pasta by hand. Whichever method you choose, it's important that the dough is not overworked; it is also essential to rest the pasta before rolling it out. It's worth investing in a pasta machine to use at home—they are inexpensive, take all the effort out of rolling, and will last for years.

Makes about 1 ¼ lb [550 g]

3 ⅓ cups [400 g] "00" pasta flour

A small pinch of salt

1 organic free-range medium egg

11 organic free-range medium egg yolks

Put the flour and salt into a food processor and turn the motor on. Add the whole egg followed by the yolks, one at a time, through the funnel, allowing each to be incorporated into the flour before adding the next. Once all the eggs are incorporated, stop the motor and gather the dough from the bowl—it may look slightly dry and crumbly but it will come together and form a ball easily if you press it in your hands. Wrap in plastic wrap and rest in the refrigerator at least 30 minutes before rolling out.

Flatten the dough with a rolling pin to the width of your pasta machine. Working in small amounts, no more than 7 oz [200 g] at a time, pass the dough through the machine on its widest setting, in one movement.

Lightly dust one side of the pasta sheet with flour and fold each end in, so they meet in the middle with the floured side on the outside. Press the edges together. Roll the pasta through the machine 4 or 5 times, narrowing the setting each time, until you reach the narrowest setting (or one earlier for stuffed pasta). Feed the pasta seam side first into the rollers and flour the sheets lightly between each rolling.

The rolled out pasta should feel smooth and elastic. Let dry 10 minutes before cutting but no longer, or it may become too dry and brittle to work with. You can now do with the pasta what you like. For ribbon pasta, fit the appropriate cutter on the machine and pass it through. Lay the strands on a sheet of parchment paper to prevent tangling.

Pappardelle with oxtail ragu

I love to eat thick ribbon pasta with an unctuous rich-tasting sauce, such as this one. Flavor is extracted from the oxtail bone during cooking and the bone marrow lends a wonderful gloss and body. To me, this is the ultimate comfort food. The sauce can be made a couple of days ahead and tastes all the better for it. If you prefer, you can cook it in a low oven at 285°F [140°C], rather than on the stovetop, in a roasting tray, tightly covered with foil.

For the ragu, put the pieces of oxtail in a large cooking pot, cover with cold water, and bring to a boil over high heat (this will help to remove any impurities). Immediately take off the heat, drain the oxtail, and set aside.

Heat the olive oil in a heavy-based saucepan (large enough to hold the oxtail) over medium heat. Add the chopped vegetables and sweat 5 minutes. Crumble in the chilies and add the garlic and herbs. Sweat over a gentle heat a further 15 minutes, stirring from time to time, until the vegetables are softened, sweet, and translucent.

Turn up the heat to high, pour in the wine, and add the tomatoes. Bring to a boil and add the blanched oxtail pieces, then immediately turn the heat down to low. Cover and cook, stirring from time to time, 2½ to 3 hours until the meat is meltingly tender and falling from the bone. Remove from the heat and let cool slightly.

Once cool enough to handle, pick off any meat that is still attached to the bone and put in another pan; discard the bones. Pass the sauce and vegetables through a sieve onto the meat, pressing down with the back of a ladle to extract as much juice as possible; discard the residue in the sieve. Warm the meat and sauce over low heat. Taste and adjust the seasoning—it will need a good pinch of salt.

To cook the pasta, bring a large pan of water to a boil, add salt, then the pasta and cook 3½ to 4 minutes until al dente. Drain and serve with the ragu.

Serves 4 to 6

1 quantity freshly made pappardelle (see page 71)

For the ragu

1 oxtail, jointed into 6 (ask your butcher to do this)

2 Tbsp olive oil

1 yellow onion, peeled and finely chopped

2 medium carrots, peeled and finely chopped

2 celery stalks, finely chopped

2 dried red chilies

4 garlic cloves, peeled and crushed

2 bay leaves

3 thyme sprigs

3 rosemary sprigs

1⅔ cups [400 ml] full-bodied red wine

1½ lb [700 g] good quality jarred (or canned) tomatoes, drained

Sea salt and freshly ground black pepper

Ravioli with sheep's milk ricotta and herb butter

These plump little pasta pillows are filled with a light yet luxurious filling,
cooked quickly to order, and served in a delicious herb-infused butter.
(Illustrated on previous pages.)

To make the filling, put the ricotta into a bowl with the lemon zest, marjoram, Parmesan, and some salt and pepper. Stir well to combine, then taste and adjust as necessary—it should be well seasoned and have a clean, lemony taste.

Roll out the pasta dough into a rectangle, about 16 x 8 in [40 x 20 cm]. Turn the dough so you have a long side facing you. Spoon little mounds of ricotta filling along the side closest to you at 2 in [5 cm] intervals, leaving a 1 in [3 cm] clear border along the front edge. Once all the ricotta has been positioned on the dough, bring the farthest edge over the filling to join the front edge and enclose the stuffing. Using your thumb and forefinger, press the pasta dough down firmly around the filling to seal. Now, using a sharp knife, cut through the sealed pasta into little square ravioli parcels.

Arrange the ravioli on a clean dish towel, spaced apart slightly, to allow them to dry out a little before cooking. If you like, you can make them a few hours in advance and keep them on a flat sheet that has been lightly dusted with semolina flour.

To cook, bring a large pan of water to a boil, add salt, then the ravioli, and cook 3½ to 4 minutes until al dente.

Meanwhile, for the herb butter, melt the butter in a saucepan large enough to hold all the ravioli once it is cooked. Add the sage or marjoram and season with a little salt and pepper.

Scoop the cooked ravioli from the water and add to the herb butter with 1 Tbsp of the water. Spoon the melted butter over the ravioli. Transfer to warm plates and serve at once.

Serves 8

1 quantity freshly made pasta (see page 71)

Semolina flour, to dust (optional)

For the filling

14 oz [400 g] sheep's milk ricotta

Finely grated zest of 2 lemons

4 marjoram sprigs, leaves only

1 ¼ cups [100 g] Parmesan, freshly grated

Sea salt and freshly ground black pepper

For the herb butter

½ cup [120 g] unsalted butter

20 sage or marjoram leaves

Spelt pasta with farro and pancetta

The inclusion of spelt flour lends a pleasing nutty flavor and texture to pasta dough. I like the unpretentious nature of this dish. Nurturing and simple, it is my go-to dish when I feel only a big bowl of pasta will satisfy.

Serves 4 to 6

For the pasta

1 cup [125 g] wholewheat spelt flour

1 cup [125 g] "00" pasta flour

1 organic free-range medium egg

10 organic free-range medium egg yolks

For the sauce

3½ oz [100 g] farro (I like the semi perlato variety)

1 yellow onion, peeled

1 carrot, peeled

1 celery stalk

1 Tbsp olive oil

4 fine slices of pancetta, chopped

1 dried red chili

2 garlic cloves, peeled and crushed

A small bunch flat-leaf parsley, leaves only, finely chopped

⅔ cup [50 g] Parmesan, freshly grated, plus extra to serve

Sea salt and freshly ground black pepper

Extra virgin olive oil, to finish

Make the pasta following the method on page 71 and cut it into tagliatelle.

For the sauce, rinse the farro well in a sieve under cold running water until the water runs clear. Tip into a saucepan, cover generously with cold water, and add a good pinch of salt. Bring to a boil, then lower the heat and simmer until the farro is just tender to the bite. Drain and set aside.

Finely chop the onion, carrot, and celery. Heat the olive oil in a medium saucepan over medium heat. When it is warm, add the onion, carrot, celery, and pancetta. Crumble in the chili, add the garlic with a pinch of salt, and stir well. Cook gently 20 minutes, stirring from time to time, until the vegetables are soft and sweet.

Toward the end of the cooking time, cook the pasta: bring a large pan of water to a boil, add salt, then the pasta and cook about 3½ to 4 minutes until al dente.

Add the farro and chopped parsley to the sauce and stir well. Stir through the grated Parmesan, then taste and adjust the seasoning.

Drain the pasta as soon as it is cooked and add to the farro, along with 1 Tbsp of the pasta cooking water. Toss together well and serve in warm pasta bowls, with a trickle of good olive oil and a bowl of grated Parmesan on the table.

The design

From the outset I knew I wanted a restaurant that was joyful, light, and uplifting, and I wanted it to feel feminine. I love eating in many of the big restaurants in London's West End, but to me they feel driven by a male energy—strong, dark, and grown up. I wanted guests to feel happy, relaxed, as if transported to an eternal spring as soon as they walked through the door. The food, of course, is paramount, but eating at Spring had to be about the whole experience—the room itself was so important.

I have a very specific color palette that I am drawn to. I love everything framed in white, but color is essential and texture is important too. Everything must have space and air around it so it can breathe and grow. I approach each plate of food in this way, so it seemed natural to embark on the room with the same philosophy.

I saw several designers but it was my sister, Briony, who understood my vision most clearly. She has worked as an interior designer in Australia for twenty-five years and appreciated my desire for a soft, joyful setting that was also modern and clean, but in no way frilly or "girly." The more we talked the more convinced I became that she could transform the space in the way that I wanted. I knew that she would treasure and take care of my dream like no one else.

There were practical difficulties as Briony runs a busy office in Sydney, Australia—there would be no quick visit if there was a problem on site—but I knew she would be fully committed to the project. She has always been clear and decisive, and I have great respect for her creativity. Working together has brought us closer. Miraculously, throughout the project we have managed to keep our relationship both professional and personal at the same time.

seafood

Grilled langoustine with seaweed butter

*This simple seaweed butter works really well alongside langoustines.
The langoustines must be very fresh—you will probably need to preorder them
from your fishmonger. Their flesh is so delicate that it needs the briefest
of cooking, otherwise it becomes rubbery and the flavor cannot be appreciated.
If you live close to the sea, take the time to forage your own seaweed.*

First, prepare the seaweed butter. Melt the butter very gently in a medium saucepan over low heat. Once it has melted, stir in the tamari, lime juice, garlic, and ginger. Stir well to combine, then add the seaweed and cook gently a couple of minutes. Taste and adjust the seasoning.

Preheat your grill to its highest setting. Using a sharp knife, split each langoustine in half lengthwise. Season the flesh with a little salt and drizzle with a little mild-tasting olive oil. Place, flesh side up, on the grill rack and cook 1 minute, or until the flesh is just opaque.

Transfer the langoustines to warm plates, spoon over the seaweed butter, and serve with lemon wedges for squeezing.

Serves 4 as an appetizer

12 to 20 very fresh raw langoustines

Mild-tasting olive oil, to drizzle

Sea salt and freshly ground black pepper

For the seaweed butter

1 ⅜ cups [300 g] unsalted butter

2 Tbsp tamari

Juice of 1 lime

1 garlic clove, peeled and chopped

½ Tbsp freshly grated ginger

4 tsp [20 g] hijiki or wakame seaweed, finely chopped

To serve

Lemon wedges

Scallops with white beans, fennel, and speck

Here succulent, sweet scallops are paired with the musty flavor
of earthy sage and the smoky flavor of speck—a lovely cured meat
from Alto Adige in northern Italy. Ask your fishmonger for
hand-dived scallops. (Illustrated on previous page.)

Have the scallops ready at room temperature.

For the dressing, combine the chili, olives, and olive oil in a bowl and season with a pinch of salt. Set aside.

Tip the warm, cooked beans into a bowl and season with salt and pepper. Add half the chopped sage, a squeeze of lemon juice, and the extra virgin olive oil. Toss well to combine.

Remove the fibrous outer layer of the fennel, and then slice the bulb in half lengthwise, reserving the feathery fronds for garnish. Cut each fennel half into very fine slivers and toss in a squeeze of lemon juice. Set aside.

Set a large heavy-based nonstick skillet over medium heat and add the olive oil. (If your pan isn't large enough to hold all the scallops comfortably, cook them in two batches rather than overcrowd the pan; if you do the scallops will stew rather than fry and turn a lovely golden color.)

Season the scallops lightly with salt and pepper. When the oil begins to smoke, add the scallops to the hot pan. Cook, undisturbed, 1 minute, then turn (in the same order that you put them in the pan) and cook a further 30 seconds. Remove the pan from the heat. Squeeze over the rest of the lemon juice and scatter over the remaining sage.

Spoon the warm beans onto warm plates and arrange the pan-fried scallops, speck, and fennel on top. Add a generous drizzle of the chili and olive dressing, finish with the fennel fronds and serve at once.

Serves 4

20 scallops, shelled and cleaned

7 oz [200 g] warm cooked small white beans, such as cannellini, drained

8 sage leaves, chopped

Juice of 1 lemon

1 Tbsp fruity extra virgin olive oil

1 fennel bulb (with feathery fronds)

1 Tbsp olive oil, for frying

1 dried chili

8 slices of speck

Sea salt and freshly ground black pepper

For the dressing

1 red chili, seeded and finely diced

12 little black olives, pitted and roughly chopped

⅓ cup [80 ml] mild-tasting olive oil

Squid with peas and sage

This light, summery combination of peas and sage is best eaten with grilled bread, rubbed with garlic, and drizzled with the fruitiest of olive oil. Look for squid that are small in size and make sure you cook them quickly over the very highest heat so that their flesh remains tender. Piping hot and well seasoned, this dish tastes and smells of a blistering hot summer's day spent close to the shore.

Serves 4

1 ¾ lb [800 g] very fresh small squid

3 Tbsp [40 g] unsalted butter

8¾ oz [250 g] freshly podded peas

1 garlic clove, peeled and crushed

3 sage sprigs

4 tsp dry white wine

A little olive oil, for cooking

Sea salt and freshly ground black pepper

Start by preparing the squid. Hold the body with one hand and pull out the head with the tentacles attached, using the other hand; most of the innards will come out too. Cut the tentacles from the head just below the eyes and discard the head. Remove the transparent quill from the body and any debris, then rinse the body pouch under cold running water. Remove the skin from the squid, which will come away easily with your fingers.

Rinse the tentacles well and leave whole. If the squid are really small, leave the pouches whole, otherwise cut in them half slightly on the diagonal. Set aside in a colander.

Put a heavy-based skillet over medium heat, then add the butter and allow to melt. When the butter starts to foam, add the peas, garlic, and sage. Stir once or twice, then turn up the heat and add the wine. Cook 2 to 3 minutes to reduce slightly.

Meanwhile, heat another heavy-based (ideally nonstick) skillet over high heat. Season the squid well with salt and pepper. Add the oil to the hot pan, then the squid pouches. Fry, without turning, a minute or so, until golden brown on the underside, adding the tentacles after about 30 seconds. Now turn the squid pouches and tentacles and color the other side for no longer than 1 minute.

Add the squid to the peas and toss well to combine. Discard the sage sprigs, then divide among warm bowls and serve.

Turbot with porcini and bone marrow

The idea for this dish was inspired by Judy Rodgers' beautiful Zuni Cafe Cookbook—a treasured book that has motivated me more than any other. Sadly, I only had the privilege of meeting Judy once, when she came to eat at Petersham. I'd like to think she would have approved of this dish.

Turbot is a robust and mighty fish. Rich and refined in flavor, it can easily hold its own alongside the luxurious, earthy porcini sauce.

First, make the sauce. Soak the porcini in a cup of warm water 10 minutes. Put half of the butter in a small heavy-based pan with the bone marrow. Put over low heat 5 minutes or until melted (you don't want it to color).

Remove the porcini from the water, reserving the liquor, and chop them fairly roughly. Add the porcini to the pan with the garlic and cook a couple of minutes. Increase the heat slightly and add the breadcrumbs and a generous grinding of pepper. Stir well to coat the crumbs in the fat.

Now add the stock and a little of the reserved porcini liquor. Cook gently a couple of minutes, stirring once or twice only, and adding a little more porcini liquor if needed but not too much. Add the Parmesan, chopped parsley, lemon zest, and a squeeze of lemon juice. Season with salt and pepper to taste. Finally, stir in the remaining knob of butter and remove from the heat.

Preheat the oven to 350°F [180°C]. Place a nonstick ovenproof skillet, large enough to hold the fish comfortably, over high heat and add the oil. When it is just smoking, season the fish all over and lay skin side down in the pan. Cook 2 minutes, without moving, until browned then turn and brown the other side 2 minutes. Transfer the pan to the middle shelf of the oven and cook a further 5 minutes.

While the fish is in the oven, reheat the sauce gently. Once cooked, transfer the turbot tranches to warm plates, spoon the sauce on top, and serve with lemon wedges.

Serves 4

2¼ lb [1 kg] very fresh turbot, cut into 8¾ oz [250 g] tranches, top skin removed

1 Tbsp olive oil

Sea salt and freshly ground black pepper

For the sauce

6 to 8 dried porcini mushrooms

3 Tbsp [40 g] unsalted butter

2 Tbsp bone marrow

1 garlic clove, peeled and crushed

1 cup [120 g] day-old sourdough breadcrumbs

1⅛ cups [250 ml] light chicken or beef stock

3 Tbsp freshly grated Parmesan

A bunch flat-leaf parsley, leaves only, finely chopped

Finely grated zest of 1 lemon

Juice of ½ lemon

To serve

Lemon wedges

Wild salmon with preserved lemon butter

*I cook fish very simply, to appreciate its superb qualities. Invariably, I leave
the skin on, as a well cooked skin—beautifully colored with a definite bite—is
the perfect counterpart to the sweet delicate succulent flesh beneath.
We cook most firm-fleshed fish the same way: skin side down in a hot pan with
a little olive oil, without turning or prodding until the skins pops from the base
of the pan. Then, still unturned, we finish the cooking in a hot oven for a minute
or two. Cooked this way, the flesh stays delicate, plump, and very pure.*

First prepare the flavored butter. Put the butter in a bowl and beat with a wooden spoon until really soft and light. Add the chopped herbs and preserved lemon and stir well until evenly incorporated. Spoon the butter onto a sheet of baking parchment and shape to form a log, enclosing the butter roll in the paper. Twist the ends of the paper to seal, then refrigerate a couple of hours.

When ready to eat, preheat the oven to 350°F [180°C]. Put a nonstick ovenproof skillet, large enough to hold the salmon fillets comfortably, over medium heat and add the oil. When the oil is just smoking, season the fish all over with salt and pepper and lay the fillets, skin side down, in the pan. Cook 2 minutes, without turning, then transfer the skillet to the middle shelf of the oven and cook a further 3 minutes.

Remove from the oven (remembering to protect your hand as the pan handle will be very hot) and put the fish fillets on warm plates, skin side up.

Put a generous slice of the flavored butter on top of the salmon and allow it to sit and slightly melt a couple of minutes before serving.

Serves 4

4 wild salmon fillets (with skin), about 7 oz [200 g] each

1 Tbsp olive oil

Sea salt and freshly ground black pepper

For the preserved lemon butter

¾ cup [160 g] unsalted butter, softened

2 tsp thyme leaves, chopped

2 tsp finely chopped flat leaf-parsley

1 Tbsp chopped preserved lemon

Sea bass with roasted tomatoes and girolles

I first cooked this dish for a gastronomic event to raise funds for
Action Against Hunger in 2013, when I was asked to make the fish course.
I wanted to keep it uncomplicated and serve it with two of my favorite
ingredients: delicate girolles and flavorful datterini tomatoes.

Serves 4

4 line-caught wild sea bass fillets (with skin), about 7 oz [200 g] each

1 Tbsp olive oil

Sea salt and freshly ground black pepper

For the roasted tomatoes

10½ oz [300 g] datterini tomatoes (or any little ripe tomato)

4 tsp red wine vinegar

Olive oil, to drizzle

For the marjoram oil and girolles

A bunch marjoram, leaves only

Finely grated zest and juice of 1 lemon

7 Tbsp [100 ml] extra virgin olive oil

12¼ oz [350 g] girolles, cleaned with a soft brush or damp cloth

3 Tbsp [40 g] unsalted butter

For the tomatoes, preheat the oven to 350°F [180°C]. Using a small knife, make a slit in each tomato, then put them in a small roasting tray. Season with salt, pepper, and the wine vinegar, drizzle over a little olive oil and toss to combine. Roast on the middle shelf of the oven 25 to 30 minutes until soft but still holding their shape. Remove and set aside.

For the marjoram oil, using a mortar and pestle, pound the herb leaves with a good pinch of salt to a rough paste. Squeeze over a little lemon juice, add the extra virgin olive oil, and stir together to make a lovely verdant sauce; set aside.

To cook the girolles, melt the butter in a nonstick saucepan over medium heat. When it begins to sizzle, add the girolles and cook 3 to 4 minutes, until they begin to soften and color, stirring only occasionally. Season with salt and pepper, and add the remaining lemon juice.

Place a nonstick ovenproof skillet, large enough to hold the fish fillets comfortably, over medium-high heat and add the 1 Tbsp oil. When hot, season the fish generously on the skin side only and lay, skin side down, in the pan. Cook 3 minutes, without turning, then transfer the pan to the middle shelf of the oven and cook a further 2 minutes.

Meanwhile, return the girolles to the heat and add the lemon zest and roasted tomatoes. Warm through gently.

Put the fish fillets on warm plates, skin side up, arrange the girolles and tomatoes alongside, and spoon over the marjoram oil. Serve at once.

Halibut with mustard seeds, curry leaves, and tomatoes

This beautiful dish presents crisp-skinned, fresh white fish in a light and aromatic broth. It is important to use whole spices here, as their flavor is cleaner, lighter, and zingier than ground spices. The tamarind adds a delicate sourness and fresh curry leaves lend an incomparable citrusy and delicately aromatic flavor. Both tamarind and curry leaves are available from Asian food stores and some grocery stores.

For the aromatic broth, put a large, heavy-based pan over medium heat. When hot, add the mustard, cardamom, and fennel seeds and toast gently, stirring, a minute or until they begin to jump from the base of the pan. Turn down the heat slightly and add the ghee (or butter), onions, ginger, and a little salt. Cook gently 15 minutes until the onions are soft and translucent. Add the curry leaves, sliced chilies, and tamarind water and cook 5 minutes. Now add the tomatoes and cook a further 20 minutes, stirring every now and then.

Meanwhile, preheat the oven to 350°F [180°C]. To cook the fish, place a large nonstick ovenproof pan over high heat, then add the butter. Season the fish generously with salt on the skin side only. When the butter is melted and sizzling, lay the fish, skin side down, in the pan and cook a couple of minutes until the skin is golden. Without turning the fish, transfer the pan to the middle shelf of the oven and cook a further 3 to 4 minutes until the fish is just cooked.

Taste the broth and adjust the seasoning—it may need a little more salt. Spoon the broth into warm bowls and lay the fish fillets on top. Scatter the curry leaves and sliced chili to taste over the dish and serve with lime wedges. I really enjoy eating this dish accompanied by steamed Asian greens or spinach and a little bowl of steamed jasmine rice.

Note To make tamarind water, soak pieces of tamarind pod in hot water to cover 15 to 20 minutes, then strain. The water will have taken on the tamarind flavor.

Serves 5

2¼ lb [1 kg] wild halibut fillet (with skin), cut into 7 oz [200 g] portions

A knob of unsalted butter

Sea salt

For the aromatic broth

1½ tsp black mustard seeds

5 cardamom pods, seeds extracted

1 tsp fennel seeds

1 Tbsp ghee (or unsalted butter)

2 small yellow onions, peeled and finely sliced

1 in [2.5 cm] knob of fresh ginger, peeled and finely sliced into matchsticks

15 fresh curry leaves

1 to 2 red chilies, seeded and finely sliced into rounds

2 Tbsp tamarind water (see note)

7 oz [200 g] ripe, flavorful tomatoes

To serve

Lime wedges

Mackerel with bread and almond sauce

*Thick, creamy, and garlicky—this sauce is a gloriously punchy
accompaniment for almost any grilled oily fish. Here I've paired it with mackerel,
but it would work equally well with sardines or anchovies. Serve the dish with
seasonal greens or a simple salad of ripe tomatoes, olives, and oregano.*

Serves 4

4 medium mackerel, scaled
and gutted

Sea salt and freshly ground
black pepper

For the sauce

⅔ cup[80 g] blanched
almonds

4¼ oz [120 g] good quality
day-old bread, crusts
removed

5 garlic cloves, peeled and
roughly chopped

1 dried red chili

2 Tbsp marjoram leaves

1⅛ cups [250 ml] extra
virgin olive oil, plus a little
extra to serve

Finely grated zest and juice
of 1 lemon

To serve

Sliced red chili

Lemon wedges

Wilted spinach

First, make the sauce. Preheat the oven to 350°F [180°C].
Scatter the almonds on a baking sheet and roast on the
middle shelf of the oven 5 minutes—to bring out their nutty
sweet flavor, rather than brown them. Remove from the
oven and set aside to cool.

Tear the bread into pieces, place in a bowl, and pour on
about 1¼ cups [300 ml] cold water. Leave to soak a couple of
minutes, then squeeze out excess water using clean hands.

Put the almonds and bread in a food processor along with
the garlic, chili, and marjoram. Whiz until combined, then
with the motor running, slowly pour in the extra virgin olive
oil through the funnel. Once all the oil is incorporated, add
the lemon juice and 1 Tbsp warm water. Taste and adjust the
seasoning, adding a little more salt or lemon juice if you
think it is necessary. You can also add a little more warm
water if you would like a slightly thinner consistency.

When ready to cook the fish, preheat the grill to its highest
setting. Rinse the mackerel inside and out. Slash each fish
3 or 4 times on each side and season inside and out with salt
and pepper. Put on the grill rack and cook under the grill
4 minutes on each side.

Transfer the grilled mackerel to warm plates. Add a generous
spoonful of the garlicky sauce, a few chili slices, and a trickle
of extra virgin olive oil. Serve at once, with lemon wedges
for squeezing and wilted spinach.

The walls

The restaurant walls were vast and needed to be filled in some way, but I was reluctant to hang paintings as I wanted to keep the room light-filled and spare. Valeria Nascimento's porcelain creations, inspired by the natural world, seemed to offer the perfect solution.

Valeria's exquisite design of tiny fine ceramic petals uncurling themselves on the walls of the restaurant seem to capture the essence of Spring more than a hundred images. In all, 4,800 blossoms adorn the walls, their shadows casting as many interesting shapes as the blossoms themselves. I see them as a celebration of the optimism and hope that the restaurant symbolizes for us.

As you enter the reception area, covering the left wall is a huge painted sheet of glass, created by Emma Peascod. The art form, known as verre églomisé, is the technique of laying paint and silver and gold leaf on the reverse side of glass. If you look closely, you will see a series of large overblown flowers, slightly out of focus. The work took over six months to complete.

meat

Guinea fowl with farro and parsley cream

I cooked this dish for a dinner at the Ballymaloe Literary Festival a couple of years ago, on Darina Allen's request, and it was well received. Full of friends from all over the world, it was a lovely evening and holds a special place in my memory, so I have a soft spot for this dish.

Have the guinea fowl supremes ready to cook. Cut the carrots and celery into chunky slices on the diagonal. Heat 1 Tbsp olive oil in a saucepan, add the carrots and celery, and cook gently, without browning, 5 minutes. Now add the farro and pour in enough water to just cover. Cook 20 minutes or until the farro and vegetables are just tender to the bite.

Meanwhile, for the parsley cream, strip the leaves from the parsley. Rinse the stalks and put in a small pan. Pour over the cream and bring to a simmer over medium heat. Turn off the heat, leave to infuse 15 minutes, then strain.

Plunge the parsley leaves into a small pan of boiling water, drain immediately, and refresh under cold water. Chop the blanched parsley very finely and set aside.

Preheat the oven to 425°F [220°C]. Season the guinea fowl well with salt and pepper. Place a nonstick ovenproof pan over high heat and add the remaining olive oil. When very hot, add the supremes, skin side down, and cook, without moving, 5 minutes until the skin is golden brown and quite crisp. Transfer to the middle of the oven and cook 12 minutes.

Meanwhile, add the wine vinegar, butter, and chopped parsley to the farro and vegetables, season well, and warm through. Warm the parsley cream over low heat and add the nutmeg, blanched parsley, and salt and pepper to taste.

To serve, divide the vegetables and farro between warm plates. Arrange the guinea fowl alongside the vegetables and spoon the parsley cream over the top. Serve at once.

Serves 4

4 guinea fowl supremes

3 carrots, peeled

2 inner celery stalks (the paler stalks around the heart)

2 Tbsp olive oil

5 oz [140 g] farro (or spelt), well rinsed

1 Tbsp red wine vinegar

2 Tbsp [30 g] unsalted butter

2 Tbsp chopped flat-leaf parsley

Sea salt and freshly ground black pepper

For the parsley cream

A large bunch flat-leaf parsley

14 Tbsp [200 ml] heavy cream

A few gratings of fresh nutmeg

Grouse with corn purée and roast figs

*I prefer grouse early in the season when their flavor is sweeter and milder
than a little later in the year. The accompanying sweet, young corn
and plump, roasted figs work beautifully with these young grouse.
Later in the year, when their flavor is more intense, I pair the birds with
more robust flavors, such as porcini, barolo, and smoky meats.*

Serves 4

4 grouse, plucked and cleaned

4 garlic cloves, peeled

8 large thyme sprigs

⅔ cup [50 g] unsalted butter

1⅛ cups [250 ml] sweet red wine, such as valpolicella

Sea salt and freshly ground black pepper

For the corn purée

2 corn cobs, outer husks removed

1⅛ cups [250 ml] milk

1 red chili, seeded and roughly chopped

2 tsp golden superfine sugar

2 Tbsp [30 g] unsalted butter

2 Tbsp crème fraîche

For the figs

8 ripe figs

4 thyme sprigs

1 Tbsp olive oil

3 Tbsp vincotto

1½ Tbsp [20 g] unsalted butter

First, make the corn purée. Stand the corn upright, pointed end down, on a board and strip the kernels from the cobs by running a sharp knife from top to bottom. Put the kernels in a saucepan with the milk, chili, sugar, and a good pinch of salt. Top up with enough water to just cover the corn. Bring to a boil over medium heat, then lower the heat and simmer until the corn is tender, about 15 minutes. Drain, saving 2 Tbsp of the cooking liquid.

Purée the corn with the reserved liquor in a blender until smooth, then strain through a fine-meshed sieve and return to a clean pan. Add the butter and crème fraîche and warm over low heat until the butter is absorbed. Taste and adjust the seasoning, adding more salt and a little pepper; the purée should be well seasoned.

Preheat the oven to 350°F [180°C]. Slice or tear the figs in half and place them in a roasting tin. Scatter over the thyme, season with a little salt and pepper, and drizzle over the oil and vincotto. Cook on the middle shelf of the oven until the figs are just soft and have begun to ooze a little of their juice. Remove from the oven and add a knob of butter. Stir gently, allowing the butter to melt into the cooking juices. Set aside.

Turn the oven up to 400°F [200°C]. Season the grouse inside and out with salt and pepper and add a garlic clove and 2 sprigs of thyme to each cavity. Put a skillet over medium heat and add the butter. When it is hot, color the grouse, 2 at a time, until browned all over. Transfer to a roasting tin.

Add the wine to the pan, turn up the heat, stir to deglaze, and let the liquor bubble to reduce by half. Pour this liquor over the grouse and roast in the oven 15 minutes. Remove from the oven and leave the birds to rest in a warm place while you reheat the figs and warm the corn purée gently over low heat.

To serve, spoon the corn purée onto warm plates. Lay the grouse alongside and finish with the figs and their juices.

Braised kid with squash, tamarind, and chickpeas

*Goat is an underused meat with a wonderful rich, almost earthy, flavor.
I like the legs and shoulders best—slowly braised with spices until meltingly tender
and falling apart. If kid is difficult to find you can substitute lamb—the flavor
is not dissimilar.*

Preheat the oven to 320°F [160°C]. Put a large skillet over medium heat. Season the meat well with salt and pepper. When the pan is hot, add the olive oil, then the meat and brown well on all sides, turning as necessary.

Transfer the meat to a roasting tin. Pour on the wine, add the garlic, and scatter over the bay leaves, dried chili, cinnamon, and star anise. Cover the tin with foil, sealing well. Cook in the middle of the oven 3½ hours, turning the meat once or twice, until tender and falling from the bone. Uncover and leave until cool enough to handle, then lift the meat onto a board and remove the bones. Return the meat to the roasting tin and add the chickpeas. Recover with the foil and return to the oven 1 hour.

Meanwhile, to prepare the squash, halve lengthwise, scoop out the seeds, then slice into wedges and put in a bowl. Toast the spice seeds in a small dry skillet over medium heat. As soon as they begin to pop, take off the heat. Pound the toasted spices finely with the dried chili flakes, using a mortar and pestle. For the dressing, put the tamarind paste in a bowl, add the ground spices, honey, lime juice, olive oil, and a good pinch of salt, and stir well to combine.

Spoon the dressing over the squash and toss to coat the wedges. Transfer them to a roasting tray, cover with foil, and put in the oven alongside the meat for the last 35 minutes of its roasting time.

Meanwhile, in a small bowl, mix the yogurt with the garlic, lime juice, and a good pinch of salt.

Check that the squash is tender by piercing with a knife. To serve, arrange the meat, squash, and chickpeas on warm plates and add a spoonful of yogurt. Scatter over the herbs and finish with a trickle of extra virgin olive oil.

Serves 4 to 6

1 kid shoulder, about 9 lb [4 kg]

1 to 2 Tbsp olive oil

1¼ cups [300 ml] dry white wine

1 garlic bulb, halved horizontally

4 to 5 bay leaves

1 dried chili, roughly chopped

2 cinnamon sticks

3 star anise

8¾ oz [250 g] cooked jarred or good quality canned chickpeas, drained

Sea salt and freshly ground black pepper

For the squash

1 winter squash (onion squash is my favorite)

½ tsp cumin seeds

½ tsp nigella seeds

½ tsp mustard seeds

½ tsp coriander seeds

½ tsp dried chili flakes

2 Tbsp tamarind paste

1 tsp honey

Juice of ½ lime

4 Tbsp olive oil

To serve

14 Tbsp [200 ml] Greek-style yogurt

2 garlic cloves, peeled and crushed

Juice of 1 lime

Herb leaves, such as sage, marjoram and/or parsley

Extra virgin olive oil, to trickle

Lamb cutlets with roasted red bell peppers and salsa verde

*I love lamb cutlets. There is something about a few sweet little bites
of tender meat attached to a bone that I find irresistible. It's that sucking
and gnawing on the bones where there is so much flavor that is
so appealing—I love quail for the same reason. Lamb lends itself well to
Middle Eastern flavors as well as anchovies and I have included
them both here. Allow 3 to 4 cutlets per person.*

Serves 4

12 to 16 little lamb cutlets, French-trimmed (ask your butcher to do this)

A little extra virgin olive oil

½ lemon

Sea salt and freshly ground black pepper

For the roasted bell peppers

2 red bell peppers

1 garlic clove, peeled and chopped

A small bunch oregano

2 anchovies, roughly chopped

1 dried chili

12 ripe little tomatoes, such as datterini

2 Tbsp olive oil

For the salsa verde

1 Tbsp cumin seeds

A bunch mint, leaves only

A bunch basil, leaves only

A bunch flat-leaf parsley, leaves only

A bunch arugula leaves

½ Tbsp Dijon mustard

2 anchovies

½ Tbsp capers (preferably packed in salt)

1 garlic clove, peeled and roughly chopped

2 Tbsp red wine vinegar

14 Tbsp [200 ml] extra virgin olive oil

First, prepare the roasted bell peppers. Preheat the oven to 400°F [200°C]. Halve the bell peppers lengthwise, scrape out and discard the seeds and white pith, then slice into quarters and place in a bowl. Add the garlic, oregano sprigs, chopped anchovies, dried chili, and a small pinch of salt. Pierce each tomato once with a small knife and add to the bowl. Trickle over the olive oil and toss to combine. Transfer everything to a roasting tray and cover it tightly with foil. Cook on the middle shelf of the oven 20 minutes, then uncover and roast a further 15 minutes or until the bell peppers are tender but still holding their shape. Remove and set aside.

To make the salsa verde, toast the cumin seeds in a small, dry pan over medium heat a minute or so until they start to pop. Tip into a mortar and grind with the pestle to a fine paste. Put the herbs and arugula into a food processor and add the mustard, anchovies, capers, garlic, and wine vinegar. Blitz briefly to chop and combine the ingredients, then with the motor running, slowly pour in the olive oil through the funnel. Once it is incorporated, transfer to a bowl and stir in the cumin. Taste and adjust the seasoning if necessary; the anchovies and capers should provide enough salt.

Lay the lamb cutlets on a board, cover with a sheet of oiled baking parchment, and pound gently with a rolling pin. Heat a griddle pan over the highest possible heat. Uncover the cutlets and season well with salt and pepper. When the pan is smoking hot, cook the cutlets, in batches as necessary, 1 to 2 minutes on each side, pressing down on them as they cook. They must be pink in the middle. Take off the heat and drizzle with a little olive oil and a squeeze of lemon.

Divide the cutlets among warm plates, arrange the roasted peppers alongside, and spoon a little salsa verde over the meat. Serve at once.

Butterflied lamb with roasted beets and carrots

*We often have grilled lamb on the menu at Spring—in one guise
or another. Sometimes we rub the surface with spices to give it a lovely
Middle Eastern feel, which works so well with the flavor created
from the flames on the grill. Here the lamb is just really well seasoned
on the outside, allowing the sweet, earthy flavors of young carrots
and beets to shine through.*

Cut the lamb into 6 portions. Mix the garlic, thyme, 4 Tbsp olive oil, and the lemon juice together in a bowl large enough to hold the lamb. Add the lamb and turn to coat well. Cover and leave to marinate at least 2 hours, turning occasionally.

Meanwhile, prepare the vegetables and sauce. Preheat the oven to 400°F [200°C]. For the sauce, roughly chop the olives and mint, combine in a bowl, and add the olive oil, wine vinegar, and a good pinch of salt. Stir well and set aside.

Put the beets on a baking sheet, drizzle with 2 Tbsp olive oil, and season with salt and pepper. Cover the sheet tightly with foil and cook on the middle shelf of the oven 30 minutes. Add the carrots to the sheet, toss with the beets, and roast, uncovered, 35 minutes or until both carrots and beets are tender when pierced with a sharp knife.

In the meantime, tear the tomatoes in half with your hands and put them in a bowl. Add the chopped rosemary and 1 Tbsp olive oil, season with salt and pepper, and toss to mix. Once the roasted vegetables are cooked, remove from the oven and add the tomatoes. Toss to combine; keep warm.

To cook the lamb, turn the grill to high. Remove the meat from the marinade, pat dry, and season well. Grill a few minutes, turning as necessary to brown well all over, then turn the heat to low and cook 6 minutes on each side. Remove and set aside in a warm place to rest 10 minutes.

Slice the lamb and arrange on warm plates with the roasted vegetables. Spoon over some olive and mint sauce to serve.

Serves 6

A leg of spring lamb, about 4½ lb [2 kg], boned and butterflied (ask your butcher to do this)

4 garlic cloves, smashed but not peeled

6 thyme sprigs

7 Tbsp olive oil

Juice of 1 lemon

A bunch of beets, scrubbed and halved lengthwise

A bunch of carrots, scrubbed and larger ones halved lengthwise

5 to 6 ripe tomatoes

3 rosemary sprigs, leaves only, chopped

Sea salt and freshly ground black pepper

For the olive and mint sauce

3½ oz [100 g] pitted good quality black olives

A bunch mint, leaves only

7 Tbsp [100 ml] olive oil

2 Tbsp red wine vinegar

Slow-cooked pork with Jerusalem artichokes, and walnut and parsley sauce

I have always loved the classic Italian slow-cooked loin of pork cooked in milk, a version of which featured in The River Café Cookbook. *Over the years I've added little touches of my own—here verjuice and a little dried chili for warmth. The sauce does not reduce to curdy morsels in the usual manner but is delicious in a different way. The rich, sticky, nutty taste of Jerusalem artichokes complements the dish beautifully.*

Serves 8

4½ lb [2 kg] piece of organic, boned young pork loin

2 Tbsp olive oil

1½ Tbsp [20 g] unsalted butter

A bunch sage, leaves only

3 bay leaves

3 garlic cloves, peeled and halved

1 dried red chili

2⅛ cups [500 ml] verjuice

4½ cups [1 L] organic whole milk

Finely pared zest of 2 lemons

Sea salt and freshly ground black pepper

For the Jerusalem artichokes

2¼ lb [1 kg] Jerusalem artichokes

A splash of olive oil

A small bunch oregano, leaves only

12 little ripe plum tomatoes, such as datterini

For the walnut sauce

20 young walnuts

2 good quality anchovy fillets (ideally Ortiz)

1 dried red chili, finely chopped

1 garlic clove, peeled and roughly chopped

A small bunch flat-leaf parsley, leaves only, chopped

14 Tbsp [200 ml] extra virgin olive oil

Preheat the oven to 350°F [180°C]. To prepare the Jerusalem artichokes, scrub them under cold running water, halve lengthwise, and put on a baking sheet. Season with salt and pepper, drizzle over the olive oil, add the oregano, and toss lightly together. Roast on the middle shelf of the oven 45 minutes, or until the artichokes are golden brown and tender through to the middle, adding the little tomatoes halfway through cooking.

For the sauce, crack the walnuts open and extract the nuts. Using a mortar and pestle, gently pound a handful of them, then gradually add the rest of the walnuts, the anchovies, chili, and garlic, continuing to pound. The sauce should be creamy in parts, textured in others. Stir in the parsley, then gradually incorporate the olive oil. Taste and add a small pinch of salt if you think it needs it. Set aside while you cook the pork.

Season the pork generously all over with salt and pepper. Heat the olive oil in a heavy-based pan, large enough to hold the pork, with a lid. Brown the pork well all over, then lift out. Pour off any fat from the pan.

Melt the butter in the pan and add the sage and bay leaves, garlic, and chili. Cook gently, stirring, 1 minute, then return the pork to the pan. Pour over the verjuice and milk, bring to a simmer, and add the strips of lemon zest.

Turn the heat to low and partially cover the pan with the lid. Simmer gently 1½ to 2 hours or until the meat is meltingly tender and the sauce has reduced by two-thirds. Taste and adjust the seasoning if necessary.

To serve, slice the pork and arrange on warm plates with the roasted Jerusalem artichokes alongside. Spoon over the walnut sauce and serve at once.

Spiced pork and veal meatballs with tomato sauce

*Warm, comforting, and uncomplicated, this is the kind of food I'm
happy to eat at home. I tend to make more than I need, as the meatballs
keep well and seem to taste even better after a couple of days. I like
to eat them alongside a little bowl of warm, oily chickpeas laced with
herbs, lemon, and chili, and a simple salad of leaves.*

*I often come across recipes that call for the meatballs to be browned
before they are added to the sauce but I consider this unnecessary.
In fact, it makes them less succulent.*

Put the ground pork and veal into a large bowl and add the garlic, lemon zest, marjoram, and breadcrumbs. Toast the whole spices gently in a small, dry pan 1 minute or so, just until they begin to pop. Immediately tip into a mortar and pound with the pestle until fine. Set aside half of the toasted spice mix for the tomato sauce.

Add the rest of the spice mix to the meat, along with the grated onion. Season generously with salt and add a little pepper, bearing in mind that the chili will impart plenty of heat. Using clean hands, mix together well. To check the seasoning, take a little of the mixture and shape it into a small, flat disc. Cook in a small pan with a little oil, then taste and adjust the seasoning of the mixture as you see fit.

Shape the mixture into balls of whatever size you prefer— I like larger meatballs, as they feel more generous. Set aside while you make the sauce.

To make the tomato sauce, heat the oil in a wide saucepan (large enough to hold the meatballs), over medium-low heat. Add the garlic, chili, and reserved toasted spices and sweat a couple of minutes, then add the tomatoes, bay leaves, chopped marjoram, and a good pinch of salt. Turn up the heat slightly and cook 15 minutes until the sauce has slightly reduced and the flavors have mingled.

Add the meatballs to the sauce and simmer 10 to 15 minutes, until cooked through. The meat will release a little fat into the sauce, lending richness and flavor. Taste for seasoning before serving.

Serves 4 to 6

1 ⅛ lb [500 g] ground pork

3½ oz [100 g] ground veal

2 garlic cloves, peeled and crushed

Finely grated zest of 1 lemon

3 marjoram sprigs, leaves only, chopped

1 cup [60 g] soft white breadcrumbs

2 tsp cumin seeds

2 tsp fennel seeds

2 tsp coriander seeds

2 tsp yellow mustard seeds

1 small yellow onion, peeled and grated

Sea salt and freshly ground black pepper

For the tomato sauce

2 Tbsp olive oil

2 garlic cloves, peeled and crushed

½ dried red chili, very finely chopped

Reserved toasted spices (from above)

1 ⅛ lb [500 g] good quality jarred or canned tomatoes

2 bay leaves

A small bunch of marjoram, leaves only, chopped

Veal chop with fried zucchini shoestrings and aïoli

When you are in the mood for meat, there is nothing more
delicious than a veal chop cooked simply—a good sprinkle of sea salt,
a little olive oil, and a squeeze of lemon is all that is needed.
And almost any accompaniment will work alongside. In the summer
months, I like to serve it with tender sweet batons of zucchini—veiled
in a light batter and deep-fried for a moment or two.
They act in the same way as perfectly cooked thin fries.
The unctuous garlicky dollop of aïoli on the
side is perfect for dipping.

Serves 6

6 veal chops

A little olive oil, for cooking

Sea salt and freshly ground black pepper

For the shoestring zucchini

3⅛ cups [375 g] all-purpose flour

1⅛ cups [250 ml] olive oil

1⅛ cups [250 ml] water

1 tsp smoked paprika

2 organic free-range egg whites

5 zucchini

Vegetable oil, for deep-frying

Handful sage leaves

For the aïoli

3 organic free-range egg yolks

Juice of 1 lemon

2 garlic cloves, peeled and crushed

1¼ cups [300 ml] extra virgin olive oil

First, make the aïoli. Put the egg yolks in a food processor and add the lemon juice, garlic, and a good pinch of salt. Blitz briefly to combine, then with the motor running, slowly pour in the olive oil through the funnel. When it is all incorporated and you have a thick aïoli, transfer to a bowl. (It will keep in the refrigerator 1 day.)

To make the batter for the zucchini, sift the flour into a large bowl and make a well in the center. Pour in the olive oil and half the water, then whisk to combine to a thick, smooth batter. Incorporate the remaining water and paprika. In a separate, clean bowl, whisk the egg whites until they hold stiff peaks, then fold into the batter. Refrigerate until ready to use; the batter will sit happily for a couple of hours.

When ready to cook, cut the zucchini in half. Finely slice lengthwise, then cut into fine matchsticks. Put in a bowl and pour on a little of the batter. Toss together lightly using your fingertips, ensuring that all the batons are well coated.

You will need to cook the veal in batches or in two large pans to avoid overcrowding. Put 2 large nonstick pans over high heat. When they are really hot, add the oil, then place the veal chops in the pan and cook, without moving, 4 minutes on one side until golden on the underside. Turn and cook a further 4 minutes on the other side. Remove from the pan and leave to rest in a warm place 10 minutes. Season the chops really generously on both sides.

Meanwhile, to cook the zucchini, heat the oil in a deep fryer or other suitable deep, heavy-based pan to 350°F [180°C]. Fry the zucchini matchsticks in batches 3 to 4 minutes, until just golden. Remove and briefly drain on paper towels. Lower the sage leaves into the hot oil in a basket and fry a few seconds, then remove and drain on paper towels.

Put the veal chops on warm plates with a pile of shoestring zucchini. Add a dollop of aïoli and finish with the fried sage leaves.

Fillet of beef with anchovy, brown butter, and wild greens

*The idea for this dish came from a conversation I had
with James Henry, the very talented young Australian chef whose
restaurant Bones in Paris has made everyone sit up and take notice.
We were discussing our mutual love of anchovies with meat.
He talked of pairing anchovies with butter that's been cooked until
its color deepens and its flavor has taken on a nuttiness.
I liked the idea and went away to try it. I absolutely love the
combination and have James to thank for this dish. It is not delicate
or pretty visually, but it tastes truly delicious!*

Preheat the oven to 400°F [200°C]. Season the meat really generously all over with salt and pepper. This is important, as the sea salt combined with high heat will give the beef a deliciously textural, crunchy outer coating.

Put a heavy-based skillet, large enough to hold the whole fillet, over high heat. When the pan begins to smoke, add the oil and swirl the pan to coat the base well. Add the meat and brown really well all over; this is best achieved by leaving the meat alone—if you push it around in the pan it will stew rather than form a crust. Once the meat is really well browned, transfer it to a baking sheet and put on the middle shelf of the oven to finish cooking for 5 minutes.

Meanwhile, put the butter in a heavy-based nonstick pan over high heat and allow it to melt and begin to foam. As soon as the butter begins to color (and smell deliciously nutty), add the anchovies and stir vigorously until they disintegrate and become a part of the sauce.

When the meat is cooked, remove it from the oven and set aside in a warm place to rest while you wilt the greens.

Once the anchovies have melted into the sauce and thickened it slightly, add the wine vinegar. Now add the greens and cook briefly, stirring, to just wilt the vegetables. Set aside.

To serve, cut the meat into thick slices, allowing 3 slices per person. Arrange on warm plates and spoon the sauce and wilted greens over the top. Serve at once.

Serves 4

1 ¾ lb [800 g] whole fillet of beef, trimmed

A splash of olive oil

7 Tbsp [100 g] unsalted butter

2 x 1 ¾ oz [50 g] cans anchovies (Ortiz are my favorite)

2 Tbsp red wine vinegar

2 handfuls of wild greens (or a mixture of arugula and green dandelion)

Sea salt and freshly ground black pepper

Skirt steak with kimchi

I'm addicted to the kimchi that we make—its hot, sharp, crunchy flavor makes your mouth feel alive. I couldn't eat much of it on its own though, as it is without question on the hot side. Kimchi works really well with rice and beef, in particular with skirt steak—a highly flavored well-textured cut of meat. It must be cooked for the shortest possible time in a very hot pan, though, as overcooking renders it tough and unappealing. Always ask your butcher for grass-fed, dry-aged beef.

Have the skirt steak at room temperature ready to cook. Steam or boil the rice in the usual way until tender.

Meanwhile, for the dressing, pour the tamari or soy sauce and verjuice or rice wine into a large bowl. Add the crushed garlic and stir well to combine. Set aside while you prepare the meat.

Using a mortar and pestle, pound the peppercorns until thoroughly but roughly cracked.

Put a heavy-based nonstick skillet over high heat. Once the pan is smoking hot, season the meat with the pepper and a good pinch of salt—the steak should be really well coated in the pepper, almost like a crust.

Add the oil to the pan and, once hot, add the meat. Cook, without moving, 2 minutes, then turn and cook a further 3 minutes on the underside. It is important to avoid turning and moving the meat any more than necessary, to ensure you get the lovely hard crust, which is what makes this dish so delicious.

As soon as the meat is ready, remove from the pan and put in the bowl of dressing. Turn to coat and let sit 5 minutes.

To serve, lift the meat out of the dressing, slice in half, then cut each portion lengthwise into 2 or 3 thick slices. Arrange the rice on a plate, rest the meat alongside, spoon over the dressing, and finish with a little kimchi. Serve at once.

Serves 2

14 oz [400 g] skirt steak, trimmed

3½ to 4¼ oz [100 to 125 g] white rice

¾ Tbsp black peppercorns

5 tsp mild-flavored oil, such as sunflower or corn

Sea salt

For the dressing

⅓ cup [80 ml] tamari or light soy sauce

7 Tbsp [100 ml] verjuice or rice wine

½ garlic clove, peeled and crushed

To serve

2 to 4 Tbsp kimchi (see page 152), to taste

The uniforms

I hadn't thought much about uniforms when one Saturday morning I walked into Maureen O'Doherty's eclectic and inspirational store, Egg, in Knightsbridge, London. I knew Maureen from her visits to Petersham and I was always pleased to see her because she is so full of life and energy. I explained that I was opening a restaurant in Somerset House later in the year. Immediately she offered to make the uniforms, or rather, she insisted. I was thrilled and excited but nervous that my budget wouldn't stretch to bespoke uniforms.

Before I knew it I was swathed in yards of calico. Boxes of shoes were brought from the storeroom for me to try on, swatches of fabric were handed to me to feel, and an intriguing wooden box full of tiny glass vials was opened before my eyes to reveal a color palette so beautiful, pure, and ethereal. Each little vial was filled with a different colored, dusty, and delicate powder. The colors were exquisite: vermillion, crushed raspberry, amber lime, charcoal, bruised plum, sherbet, saffron yellow, and buttered cream. I was smitten. I knew that, whatever the cost, there was no going back. The uniforms would be designed by Egg.

Working on the uniforms with Maureen and her great team has been one of the most exciting parts of the project. Her relentless enthusiasm and utter commitment breathed life into Spring (which was still in effect just drawings on paper) and made it feel real and alive. Our meetings were fun, creative and always exciting. It did, however, take several months and a lot of hard work to get to the final design.

The uniforms had to look beautiful, of course, but they also needed to be practical and comfortable. Maureen began with the design of the apron, then moved on to the other uniforms. There are many different roles on a restaurant floor: general manager, sommelier, head waiter, bar manager, receptionist, plate runners, and bar backs. All their uniforms needed to be slightly different in order to make them identifiable, but also because their roles have different requirements. Much thought had to go into the functionality of the individual attire but, most importantly, the overall design needed to feel fluid and coherent.

vegetables

Samphire and chili oil

This is a simple and pretty side to serve with roasted sea bass or salmon,
or barbecued lamb, during the months when samphire is in season.
Samphire can be salty, so resist the temptation to salt the cooking water
during cooking—and taste the vegetable before seasoning to serve.
A squeeze of lemon juice will help to counteract any slight saltiness.
Use sweet-tasting, succulent local samphire if possible.

Serves 4

1 red chili

3½ Tbsp [50 ml] extra virgin olive oil

5¼ oz [150 g] yellow wax beans

1⅓ lb [600 g] samphire

Lemon wedges, to serve

Slice the chili in half lengthwise and scrape out the seeds. Cut the chili into fine strips, then chop across the strips to give neat even shapes. Put the chopped chili in a bowl, pour over the olive oil, and stir to mix. Set aside while you cook the beans and samphire.

Bring a small pan of water to a boil, add the yellow wax beans, and cook about 3 minutes until just tender, then drain well.

In the meantime, rinse the samphire well in several changes of water and trim the base of the stems. Add the samphire to a large pan of boiling water and cook until the water returns to a boil; this should take no more than 1 minute.

Drain the samphire in a colander and toss with the beans. Pile into a warm serving dish or onto individual plates and spoon on the chili oil. Serve with lemon wedges.

Radishes poached in chicken stock and butter

*I first came across this lovely recipe in France many years ago. It is unusual
in that it calls for radishes to be cooked. I find this somewhat surprising,
but once a little heat has been applied to them their flavor is truly
delicious—nutty and elegant, retaining only a hint of their peppery nature.
I love the way their vibrant red color fades away during cooking
too, until the radishes are the palest, most beautiful pink.
A stylish accompaniment to roast chicken or poached white fish.*

Remove the stalks from the radishes and wash thoroughly
in cold water. Shake dry and place in a heavy-based medium
pan that is large enough to comfortably hold the radishes
and their cooking liquid.

Pour over the chicken stock and add the butter (don't worry
if the liquid doesn't completely cover the radishes). Add a
small pinch of salt and place over medium heat. Bring to a
boil, then turn down the heat to a gentle simmer. Cook until
the radishes are almost tender, tossing them once or twice
to coat in the cooking liquor; this should take no more than
8 minutes.

When the radishes are almost tender, turn up the heat
slightly to reduce the liquor down until there is just enough
to coat the radishes in a pale, glossy glaze. Spoon the radishes
into a warm bowl, add a sprinkling of salt and a generous
grinding of pepper and serve.

Serves 6

2 bunches of breakfast
radishes

14 Tbsp [200 ml] chicken
stock

4½ Tbsp [60 g] unsalted
butter

Sea salt and freshly ground
black pepper

Broccoli with garlic, chili, and black olive dressing

*I like to make this recipe when the first tender, young broccoli of the year
appears. It is every bit as delicious as the new season's asparagus.
The fine green stems are particularly succulent, so don't be tempted to cut
these short. Here, the broccoli is quickly blanched, then sautéed with
a little garlic and some red chili. Serve as an accompaniment
to grilled meat or fish, or with some young goat's curd and warm, crusty
peasant style bread as a light lunch.*

Serves 4

1 ½ lb [700 g] young tenderstem broccoli

2 Tbsp olive oil

2 garlic cloves, peeled and finely chopped

1 red chili, halved lengthwise, seeded and finely chopped

Juice of ½ lemon

Sea salt

For the olive dressing

A small bunch flat-leaf parsley, leaves only

2 Tbsp good quality black olives, stoned (I like the little Ligurian ones)

3 ½ Tbsp [50 ml] olive oil

Finely grated zest of 1 lemon

First, make the dressing. Chop the parsley finely and the olives roughly. Put them in a bowl and pour over the olive oil, then stir in the lemon zest and a little salt to taste.

Trim the ends off the broccoli. Put a large pan of well salted water on to boil. Once the water is boiling, add the broccoli and cook just until the water returns to a boil, then drain; keep warm.

Put a sauté pan, large enough to hold the broccoli, over medium heat, then add the olive oil. When it is warm, add the garlic and chili. Cook 1 minute, just until the garlic begins to brown—don't let it burn, or it will make the dish taste bitter.

Add the broccoli and turn the stalks over once or twice to coat them with the garlic and chili, then squeeze over a little lemon juice.

Transfer to a warm plate and spoon over a little of the olive dressing, or serve the dressing in a little bowl on the side for guests to help themselves. This dish is also lovely served at room temperature.

Spinach with girolles

Come midsummer, when the first of the girolles start to trickle through,
I feel happy and content. Aside from porcini, these are my favorite mushrooms
—I love their clean, gentle, slightly woody flavor. I often serve this dish with
pigeon, as it balances the rich flavor of the meat perfectly and lends a clarity
to the final assembly. It works beautifully with beef and veal too.
It is also lovely on its own with some good bread, though you may want
to increase the quantities below (by half as much again, perhaps).

Wash the spinach well in cool water to remove any dirt trapped in the leaves. Gently shake it dry, then put in a saucepan large enough to hold all the leaves comfortably. Put over medium heat and, as soon as the spinach begins to wilt, toss it a couple of times, then remove from the heat. Drain in a colander and set aside to cool.

While the spinach is cooling, clean the mushrooms. I find the most useful tool to use is a small pastry brush. Carefully brush each girolle to remove any dirt and debris—it is important to avoid washing mushrooms to clean them because they soon become waterlogged and lose all their delicious flavor.

Put a sauté pan over medium-low heat and add the butter. Allow it to melt and foam but not brown. Add the girolles, being careful not to overcrowd the pan. Cook, without stirring, a couple of minutes, then gently toss the girolles in the pan, adding the garlic and lemon juice. Season with a good pinch of sea salt and a grinding of pepper.

Squeeze the spinach gently between the palm of your hands to remove as much liquid as possible, then add to the pan. Toss well to combine and heat until the spinach is just warmed through. Taste and adjust the seasoning, then serve.

Serves 4

7 oz [200 g] large leaf spinach

5¼ oz [150 g] girolles

2 Tbsp [30 g] unsalted butter

1 garlic clove, peeled and finely chopped

Few drops of lemon juice

Sea salt and freshly ground black pepper

Slow-cooked zucchini with tarragon

*I love this method of cooking zucchini. It is the one I return to time
and again—and the recipe I have been asked for more than any other over
the years. It works as an accompaniment with almost any dish.
Use another soft herb in place of the tarragon if you like—the zucchini will
happily partner basil, mint, parsley, or chervil. In order to achieve
the gentle unctuous flavor and texture that you are looking for,
it is essential to cook the zucchini really slowly over the gentlest possible
heat, without letting them brown.*

Trim the zucchini and slice them into fine rounds, about
⅛ in [3 mm] thick.

Put a large heavy-based pan over medium heat and add the
olive oil and butter. Once the butter has melted, add the
zucchini and stir well to coat the slices in the melted butter
and oil. Add the crushed garlic and a good pinch of salt.

Now turn the heat down to its lowest possible setting and
put a lid on the pan. Cook 40 minutes, stirring every few
minutes to ensure that the zucchini do not stick to the
bottom of the pan or brown. As the zucchini cook they will
soften and their flavor will deepen, taking on a lovely garlicky
aroma. Eventually they will begin to disintegrate, becoming
almost like a thick mushy jam.

At this point, remove from the heat and add the chopped
tarragon, plenty of pepper, and a good pinch of salt. Stir
well and serve. These zucchini are surprisingly good eaten
cold as well—often I toss them through a salad of leaves and
cooked lentils dressed with a little olive oil and wine vinegar.

Serves 6

12 small firm zucchini

3 Tbsp extra virgin olive oil

3 Tbsp [40 g] unsalted butter

2 garlic cloves, peeled and crushed

5 tarragon sprigs, leaves only, chopped

Sea salt and freshly ground black pepper

Slow-cooked chard with chickpeas

*The pairing of chickpeas with spinach or chard is a fairly classic one.
You will see versions of this dish in many guises throughout
the Middle East. A delicious and very moreish combination,
it works particularly well alongside the meatball recipe on
page 114, but I can happily eat a plateful just on its own.
It is a dish that nurtures you from the inside—real comfort food.*

Drain the chickpeas, rinse, and put them in a large heavy-based pan. Cover generously with cold water, but do not season. Bring to a boil over medium heat, then lower the heat and simmer gently until tender. This will take 1 to 1½ hours, depending on the age of the beans.

Toast the cumin seeds in a dry pan over medium heat until they just begin to pop in the pan, then remove from the heat. Pound the toasted cumin finely, using a mortar and pestle.

Put a large pot of well salted water on to boil. Once it is boiling, add the chard and cook just until the water returns to a boil, then remove from the heat and drain in a colander. Leave until the chard is cool enough to handle, then chop really finely.

Warm half the olive oil in a saucepan over low heat, then add the onion, garlic, chili, and cumin. Stir well, season with a pinch of salt, and cook over low heat 10 minutes.

Now add the chard and continue to cook a further 20 minutes or until the chard is soft and dark in color. Add the chickpeas and the rest of the olive oil. Stir well and taste: it should have a warm, spicy, and slightly sour flavor. To finish, stir in the yogurt, mint, and a squeeze of lemon juice. Serve at once.

Serves 4

8 oz [225 g] chickpeas, soaked overnight

½ tsp cumin seeds

A bunch chard, well washed

4 Tbsp extra virgin olive oil

1 large yellow onion, peeled and finely chopped

2 garlic cloves, peeled and finely chopped

1 red chili, halved lengthwise, seeded, and finely chopped

⅝ cup [150 ml] natural yogurt

4 mint sprigs, leaves only, chopped

1 Tbsp lemon juice

Sea salt

Yellow wax beans, radicchio, barley, and basil

This is really just a delicious tangle of vegetables laced with olive oil, lemon juice, and fresh herbs. Sometimes I replace the barley with little potatoes, such as Roseval or Duke of York, depending on the dish. For fish, I would say potatoes work better; with lamb, beef, or roast chicken, the barley is perfect.

Serves 4

5¼ oz [150 g] pearl barley

3½ Tbsp [50 ml] extra virgin olive oil

5¼ oz [150 g] ripe little tomatoes, such as datterini

A small bunch marjoram, leaves only

2 Tbsp red wine vinegar

A handful yellow wax beans, topped but not tailed

¾ cup [60 g] Parmesan, freshly grated

1 small radicchio, halved

A large bunch basil

Finely grated zest of 1 lemon and the juice of ½ lemon

Sea salt and freshly ground black pepper

Rinse the barley in a colander under cold running water until the water runs clear, then tip into a pan and add fresh water to cover. Bring to a boil over medium heat, then turn the heat down and simmer about 40 minutes until the barley is tender but still firm to the bite.

Meanwhile, put half the olive oil into a saucepan and place over gentle heat. When it is just warm, add the tomatoes and marjoram and cook, stirring every now and then, until the tomatoes are just soft but still holding their shape. Season with salt and add the wine vinegar.

Put a separate pan of well salted water on to boil. Once the water is boiling, add the beans and cook 2 minutes, then drain but don't refresh. Drain the barley too.

Add the beans and barley to the tomatoes, along with the Parmesan and the rest of the olive oil. Stir to combine.

Slice each radicchio half into ¾ to 1 in [2 to 3 cm] strips, then add to the pan. Tear in the basil and finish with the lemon zest and juice. Taste and adjust the seasoning if necessary. Serve warm, rather than hot.

New season's potatoes with lovage oil

*Full of personality, lovage is a strong herb, tasting a little like
celery, so I tend to use it sparingly. It is particularly good added
to a salsa verde to accompany tender young lamb in late spring
or early summer. I've also discovered that it is very nice with the first of the
year's potatoes. Here I've paired it with Jersey Royals, lightly braised
celery hearts, and radicchio, which adds color to the plate.
It works as an accompaniment to almost anything—try it with grilled
lamb, roast chicken, or the first of the season's wild salmon.*

First make the lovage oil. Put the lovage in a food processor
or blender, add the extra virgin olive oil, and a small pinch
of salt and blend until really smooth. Transfer to a bowl and
set aside.

Put a pan of well salted water on to boil. Scrub the potatoes
gently under cool running water to remove any dirt. Once
the water is boiling, add the potatoes and cook until just
tender; this will take about 20 minutes.

Finely slice the celery on the diagonal into long fine shards.
Put in a shallow pan and add the verjuice, olive oil, bay leaves,
and thyme. Pour in enough water to just cover, season with
a little salt, and put over medium heat. Bring to a boil, then
reduce the heat to a simmer. Cook until still just firm to the
bite, about 5 minutes. Drain and set aside to cool.

Pass the lovage oil through a fine strainer if you would like
a clear, verdantly green oil (or leave it unstrained for a little
texture).

Drain the potatoes as soon as they are cooked and place in
a bowl. Add the radicchio leaves and celery. Spoon the lovage
oil over the vegetables, add a little lemon juice, and toss well
to combine. Taste and adjust the seasoning before serving.

Serves 4 to 6

2¼ lb [1 kg] Jersey Royals, or
other small boiling potato,
such as Roseval, Ratte, or
Pink Fir Apple

A bunch celery (tender white
heart only)

⅝ cup [150 ml] verjuice

2 Tbsp olive oil

2 bay leaves

1 thyme sprig

1 small radicchio, leaves
separated

A little squeeze of lemon juice

Sea salt and freshly ground
black pepper

For the lovage oil

4 lovage sprigs

¾ cup [180 ml] mild-tasting
extra virgin olive oil

The garden

Having a sense of an outdoor space at the restaurant was important for me. I had worked closely with nature for so many years that the idea of giving that up completely was difficult. From my first visit to Somerset House, I focused on the space that could become a garden—the light well in the middle of the room. It needed to have a very different atmosphere from the restaurant room itself, which would be light and fresh. For a dramatic contrast, I wanted the garden to feel dark, almost dank, like an enchanted wood with a magical quality. As you stepped inside, I wanted it to feel as though you had been transported somewhere else.

I set about finding out exactly what could be done to that space. Covered with a glass roof, it was, technically, an indoor rather than an outdoor space—heated and warm in the winter, kept cool in the summer. Inevitably there would be constraints and I knew it was going to be difficult to realize my dream. It took a while to find the right garden designer, but from the moment I met Jinny Blom I knew she could deliver my vision. She understood the theatrical quality I was looking for and her extraordinary imagination impressed me.

One of my main concerns had always been the walls of the garden, which I felt needed to look aged in some way. Jinny arrived at the office one day with a large piece of drab plywood. She flipped it over to reveal the beautiful, almost primeval, shape of a gunnera leaf among some very rough plaster of Paris. Jinny's idea was to clad the walls in cast corian with a repeat pattern of the gunnera leaf. The effect would be dramatic and enchanting. I was beyond excited.

There were many challenges. Outdoor plants would never be happy inside and we needed to put a few tables and chairs out there, so the space for plants was restricted. Everything needed to be grown in pots that were movable on castors so that the room could be adapted to different occasions. Fascinated by the structure and limitations of the garden, Jinny came up with inspiring ideas and plant solutions. The garden would be ultimately beautiful. The enchanting forest of my imagination was beginning to take shape.

fermented

Pickled cucumbers

*As far back as I can remember I have loved pickled cucumbers.
My mother always had a jar in our refrigerator and we ate them as a
snack with a wedge of sharp, tangy Cheddar cheese. Here the cucumbers
are fermented using an ancient technique, known as lactose
fermentation—in a combination of whey and water, laced with spices, salt,
and dill, in an anaerobic environment. This produces good bacteria,
which in turn fight bad bacteria—so these pickled cucumbers are good for
you! Their flavor is less acidic than you might expect, but truly delicious.
Look for small bright green cucumbers with tight skins that are heavy
for their size, without bruises or blemishes.*

Wash the cucumbers and pat dry. Pack them fairly tightly into a sterilized jar, scattering the dill sprigs and mustard seeds in between them.

Put the whey, 1⅛ cups [250 ml] of the water, and the salt into a bowl and stir well to dissolve the salt and combine the whey. Pour this over the cucumbers and top up with a little extra water if necessary to ensure that the liquid reaches the top of the jar. Seal with a tight-fitting lid.

Store the jar in a cool dark place 2 to 3 days, then transfer to the refrigerator. The cucumbers are ready to eat 7 days after packing them into the jar.

Makes 1 ⅛ lb [500 g]

1 ⅛ lb [500 g] small cucumbers

A few dill sprigs

1 tsp mustard seeds

2 Tbsp whey (from making cheese, such as ricotta, see page 44)

1 ⅛ to 2 ⅛ cups [250 to 500 ml] bottled water

2 Tbsp coarse salt

Kombucha

This tea-based beverage is believed to have originated in ancient China, but I only discovered it a few years ago, on a visit to Australia. I bought a bottle from a farmers' market and was intrigued by its lively, effervescent and slightly vinegary taste. When I returned home, I decided to try making my own kombucha and bought a starter culture online—a Scoby (Symbiotic Culture of Bacteria and Yeast). It arrived in a small plastic container and looked almost like a jellyfish. I use a simple organic black tea—flavored teas often contain oils that can spoil the Scoby. Since that first attempt I've made kombucha regularly, each batch stemming from the original. (Illustrated on previous page.)

Start by washing your hands really well. This is important, to prevent any contamination.

Bring the water to a boil in a saucepan and continue to boil 5 minutes to purify. Take off the heat and add the tea bags. Let cool slightly, then add the sugar and stir well to dissolve. Set aside to cool.

Once cooled to room temperature, strain the liquid and discard the tea bags. Pour the cooled tea into a sterilized 6½ cup [1.5 L] kilner jar and stir in the kombucha. Add the Scoby and seal with a tight-fitting lid.

Leave in a warm, dark place (158°F [70°C] is ideal) 7 to 10 days. The kombucha is ready when it no longer tastes sweet, but has a gentle fizz and a distinctly vinegary taste. During this fermentation process the Scoby, which is essentially a "mother," will produce a "baby."

When the kombucha is ready, strain and discard the original Scoby, set the "baby" aside along with a little of the kombucha you have just made to start a new batch.

Decant the kombucha into smaller sterilized bottles. Fit the lids loosely and put in the refrigerator. Kombucha tastes best when served really well chilled.

Note If you would like to add flavorings you can do so after the kombucha has been fermented, before decanting it into smaller bottles. Ginger is nice, as is cardamom, though I prefer to keep it plain.

Makes 6½ cups [1.5 L]

8 cups [2 L] water

12 organic black tea bags

1½ cups [300 g] golden superfine sugar

7 Tbsp [100 ml] kombucha

1 Scoby

Sauerkraut

Real homemade sauerkraut is a world away from the sharp, astringent store-bought variety. Delightfully crunchy and sour, it is easy to make and addictive to eat. You need little equipment: a chopping board, sharp knife, and a sterilized jar and you're ready to go. If you are new to fermentation, sauerkraut is a perfect first thing to try. I prefer to make it one jar at a time, rather than in large quantities.

You can use green cabbage if you prefer but I love the vibrancy of red cabbage—and I enjoy eating food that is alluringly strong in color. Here I have added a little caraway, but you can add grated carrot, crushed garlic, or ginger if their flavors are more appealing to you.

Makes about 1 ⅓ lb [600 g]

1 red cabbage
1 ½ Tbsp coarse salt
1 Tbsp caraway seeds

Using a sharp knife, slice the cabbage in half, remove the outer leaves, and set aside. Cut out and discard the core from the cabbage. Lay the cabbage halves cut side down on a board and slice each half as finely as possible.

Put the shredded cabbage into a bowl and sprinkle over the salt and caraway seeds. Using very clean hands, massage the cabbage vigorously—this will help it soften and release its natural juice.

When the cabbage is almost wet, transfer it to a sterilized 6½ cup [1.5 L] jar, packing it in tightly until it reaches the top of the jar. Place one of the discarded outer leaves on top to help seal the cabbage and screw the lid of the jar on tightly.

Store in a cool dark cupboard—the cabbage will be ready to eat after 2 to 3 days, but it can be kept 2 to 3 months. Once opened, refrigerate and use within a few days.

Kimchi

*Hot, sour, and gloriously crunchy, kimchi is the most delicious
and moreish of condiments. I started making it in much the same way
as sauerkraut—salting the vegetables and adding a little chili and ginger.
My recipe has evolved since then, but it is the most authentic and
nicest I have come across. I can eat kimchi straight from the jar or simply
with nothing more than a little bowl of sticky steamed rice. Most of the
ingredients are readily available at a good Asian food store.*

*Makes 1 large or
2 smaller jars*

1 Chinese cabbage

3½ Tbsp [55 g] coarse salt

8 cups [2 L] water

2 Tbsp dried shrimp

4 dried anchovies

½ cup cooked white rice
(1 ¾ oz [50 g] uncooked
weight)

½ yellow onion, peeled and
chopped

1 apple, peeled, cored, and
finely sliced

1 ½ in [4 cm] piece of fresh
ginger, peeled, and chopped

5 garlic cloves, peeled, and
roughly chopped

2 Tbsp superfine sugar

3 Tbsp fish sauce

3 Tbsp dried chili flakes

1 bunch scallions, trimmed

To prepare the salted cabbage, put the salt into a stainless steel or glass bowl large enough to hold the cabbage. Pour over 6½ cup [1.5 L] water and stir well to dissolve the salt.

Slice the cabbage in half lengthwise and then cut into 2 in [5 cm] pieces. Immerse the cabbage in the salted water and leave 1 hour. Stir well, then let sit another 30 minutes.

Meanwhile, put the dried shrimp and anchovies into a small saucepan and pour on the remaining 2⅛ cups [500 ml] water. Bring to a boil over high heat, then turn down the heat and simmer 5 minutes. Remove from the heat and strain the broth into a bowl, discarding the fish.

Put the cooked rice, onion, apple, ginger, and garlic into a blender and pour over the broth. Blend thoroughly. Spoon into a bowl and add the sugar, fish sauce, and chili flakes. Stir well and let stand 10 minutes.

Drain the cabbage. Slice the scallion finely and add to the cabbage. Now add the sauce and mix together, loosely but very thoroughly, using very clean hands. Ladle into 1 large (or 2 smaller) sterilized jar(s).

Finally pour a little water into the bowl in which you have mixed the kimchi. Swish this around to gather any residue and then pour over the kimchi in the jar(s). Seal.

The kimchi will be ready to use almost straightaway (I love it newly made, as it is so vibrant and crunchy) but it will keep well up to 2 months in the refrigerator.

desserts

Iced summer fruits with rose-scented geranium syrup

Wonderfully refreshing, this is the perfect ending to a long, lazy summer lunch in the backyard under dappled light. Not too sweet, slightly ethereal in flavor, and unfussy in execution, it is the sort of dessert I like to serve. It isn't served frozen as such, it just feels cool—like ice— as it slips down your throat. Vary the fruit according to what's in season; later in the summer I use greengages in place of gooseberries.

Slice the peaches in half and remove their stones. Put in a wide heavy-based pan, in a single layer. Add the powdered sugar, geranium leaves, if using, the vanilla pod (with seeds), and enough water to just cover the fruit. Put over low heat and bring to just below a simmer. Stir once or twice, then put a lid on the pan and cook very gently 10 minutes or until the fruit is just tender when pierced with a small knife.

Meanwhile, top and tail the gooseberries. Add to the pan and cook a further 5 minutes. Remove from the heat and set aside to cool.

Once the fruit has cooled, if using rose syrup, add a little to taste. Transfer to a suitable container and place in the freezer about 45 minutes or until really well chilled.

To serve, slice the strawberries in half lengthwise. Arrange the peaches and gooseberries on chilled plates, spoon over the syrup, and add the blackberries and strawberries. Finish with a few geranium leaves and/or the vanilla pod if you like. Serve at once.

Serves 6

6 ripe, sweet peaches, unblemished and heavy for their size

⅞ cup [100 g] powdered sugar

A few sprigs rose-scented geranium leaves (Attar of Roses), or a splash of rose syrup

1 vanilla pod, split in half lengthwise

7 oz [200 g] gooseberries

7 oz [200 g] small ripe strawberries

3½ oz [100 g] ripe blackberries

Rhubarb crisp

This delicious dessert takes very little time to prepare. Strawberries and rhubarb have a great affinity with each other—the delicate fragrance of the strawberries more than holding its own against the sharp acidity of the rhubarb. Look for rhubarb with bright leaves and firm, unblemished stalks.

Preheat the oven to 400°F [200°C]. For the topping, spread the walnuts out on a sheet and toast about 5 minutes until they smell nutty and have taken on a gentle golden color. Remove from the oven and let cool. Lower the oven setting to 350°F [180°C].

Once cooled, pulse the nuts in a food processor until coarsely chopped into approximately ¼ in [5 mm] pieces (no larger or they are likely to stick out and burn).

Sift the flour and cinnamon into a large bowl and stir in the brown sugar. Add the softened butter and work in with your fingertips until you have a mixture that is crumbly but loosely holding together. Mix in the walnuts and set aside while you prepare the fruit.

Cut the rhubarb into 1 in [2.5 cm] slices. Hull the strawberries and slice half of them (the larger ones). Put the rhubarb and strawberries into a large bowl and scatter over the superfine sugar, flour, and salt. Toss together to combine and let stand a few minutes.

Spread the fruit mixture evenly in a pie dish (about 9 in [23 cm] in diameter) and smooth the surface. Sprinkle the topping over the fruit in an even layer. Cook on the middle shelf of the oven 40 to 45 minutes, or until the juices are bubbling around the edges, the rhubarb is soft, and the topping is golden brown. Serve warm, with thick cream.

Serves 6 to 8

2¼ lb [1 kg] rhubarb

7 oz [200 g] plump ripe strawberries

1⅛ cups [120 g] golden superfine sugar

3 Tbsp all-purpose flour

Small pinch of salt

For the topping

1⅓ cups [150 g] shelled walnuts

1⅔ cups [200 g] all-purpose flour

¼ tsp ground cinnamon

½ cup [100 g] soft brown sugar

6 Tbsp [80 g] unsalted butter, softened

Blackcurrant and buttermilk pudding

When we started to make butter for the restaurant, we found ourselves with a lot of buttermilk, so, rather than waste it, we came up with various uses for it, including this delightful pudding. It adds a pleasant sourness that works well with the velvety intense sharpness of blackcurrants. Lemon verbena, which grows happily in my backyard in a small sunny spot, lends a clean, ethereal taste to the pudding.

Serves 6

3 sheets of bronze leaf gelatine (2 tsp in total)

1 ⅓ cups [400 ml] heavy cream

1 ⅛ cups [220 g] superfine sugar

Finely pared zest of 1 lemon

1 vanilla pod, split in half lengthwise

2 or 3 lemon verbena sprigs

2 ⅛ cups [500 ml] buttermilk

For the blackcurrant sauce

14 oz [400 g] blackcurrants

1 cup [200 g] superfine sugar

½ cup [120 ml] water

A tiny pinch of salt

A squeeze of lemon juice

First make the sauce. Put the blackcurrants in a heavy-based pan with the sugar and water. Bring to a simmer over medium heat and cook a couple of minutes until the fruit has started to release its juices. Remove from the heat and pass half of the fruit and juice through a sieve into a bowl, pressing the fruit with the back of a spoon to extract as much juice as possible; discard the pulp. Stir the rest of the blackcurrants into the strained juice, along with the salt and a few drops of lemon juice. Let cool, then chill in the refrigerator.

To make the puddings, soak the gelatine leaves in a shallow dish of cold water to soften. Meanwhile, put the cream in a heavy-based saucepan with the sugar, lemon zest, vanilla pod, and lemon verbena. Slowly bring to a simmer over a medium heat, stirring often, then lower the heat and cook 3 minutes. Take the pan off the heat. Immediately remove the gelatine leaves from the water and stir into the hot mixture. Continue to stir until the gelatine has fully dissolved.

Strain the mixture through a fine sieve into a bowl, discarding the flavorings. Add the buttermilk and stir well.

Pour into 6 ramekins, 14 Tbsp [200 ml] capacity, to about ⅜ in [1 cm] from the top (to leave room for the blackcurrant sauce). Let cool, then refrigerate until set; this will take about 3 hours.

To serve, spoon a layer of blackcurrant sauce over the top of the puddings, to cover them completely. Serve the rest of the sauce in a bowl on the side, for everyone to help themselves to a little more if they wish to do so.

Summer pudding

*Nothing says English summer to me quite like a summer pudding,
and I return to this recipe year after year, when the beautiful soft summer
fruits are at their peak. I make a sponge rather than use the more
traditional stale bread—the extra effort is well worth it. I also use more
currants than other fruits as they keep the sweetness in check. Serve each
portion topped with a dollop of crème fraîche or thick cream.
(Also illustrated on previous pages.)*

Serves 8 to 10

For the sponge

1 Tbsp [15 g] unsalted butter, plus extra to grease

7 organic free-range medium eggs, separated

1 ⅞ cups [375 g] superfine sugar

Small pinch of salt

3 cups [360 g] all-purpose flour, sifted

5 Tbsp [75 ml] warm water

For the fruit

10½ oz [300 g] blackcurrants

10½ oz [300 g] redcurrants

1¼ cups [250 g] superfine sugar

Finely grated zest and juice of 1 lemon

7 oz [200 g] blackberries

7 oz [200 g] raspberries

3½ oz [100 g] strawberries

For the sponge, preheat the oven to 350°F [180°C] and grease a 13 x 9 in [33 x 23 cm] baking tin. Melt the butter in a small pan over low heat; let cool. Using an electric mixer, whisk the egg yolks with half the sugar until pale and thick enough to leave a ribbon trail on the surface when the whisk is lifted.

In a separate, clean bowl, whisk the egg whites with a pinch of salt and the remaining sugar, whisking slowly to begin with, then increasing the speed slightly after 1 or 2 minutes. Continue to whisk until the mixture holds stiff peaks.

Carefully fold the flour into the egg yolk and sugar mix, a third at a time, alternately with the water. Fold in the whisked whites, a third at a time. Finally, fold in the melted butter.

Spread the mixture thinly and evenly in the prepared baking tin. Bake on the middle shelf of the oven 8 to 10 minutes or until the sponge is just golden and dry to the touch. Leave in the tin a few minutes, then turn out and let cool on a wire rack while you prepare the fruit.

Place the black- and redcurrants in a saucepan with the sugar and lemon juice and cook over medium heat until the fruit just starts to release its juices. Remove from the heat and add the rest of the fruit and the lemon zest. Let stand a few minutes to allow the flavors to develop.

Line a 4½ cup [1 L] ceramic basin with plastic wrap, leaving plenty overhanging all round. Using a pastry cutter, cut 2 rounds of sponge, one to fit the bottom of the basin and one the diameter of the top. Place the smaller disc in the bottom of the basin. Now cut long, tapering strips of sponge and use to line the sides of the basin, overlapping them slightly and pressing tightly to ensure there are no gaps.

Using a slotted spoon, spoon the fruit into the sponge-lined basin, filling it to the brim. Spoon on the juices, reserving a few spoonfuls for serving. Lay the other sponge disc on top. Fold over the plastic wrap to seal and place a saucer on top that just fits inside the rim of the basin. Weigh down with a can (or something similar) and refrigerate overnight.

To serve, fold back the plastic wrap and invert the pudding onto a deep plate. Using a pastry brush, smear any pale areas of sponge with the reserved juice.

Quince and cobnut tart

Quince is probably my favorite fall fruit. Tasting somewhere between an
apricot and a pear, it is beautiful to behold and a joy to cook. It does,
however, need long, slow cooking to soften the flesh and intensify the
lovely color. This upside-down tart is really a variation
on a tarte tatin and is best eaten still slightly warm from the oven,
with a scoop of vanilla ice cream or crème fraîche.

Serves 8 to 10

For the quince

4 firm, ripe, unblemished quinces

½ cup [100 g] superfine sugar

2 bay leaves

1 vanilla pod, split in half lengthwise

About 1 ½ cups [350 ml] verjuice or water

For the pastry

1 ¼ cups [150 g] all-purpose flour

6 Tbsp [85 g] chilled unsalted butter

Pinch of salt

1 tsp superfine sugar

3 Tbsp chilled water

To assemble

⅛ cup chopped cobnuts or hazelnuts

1 ½ Tbsp [20 g] chilled unsalted butter, cut into small flakes

1 to 1 ½ Tbsp superfine sugar

Preheat the oven to 320°F [160°C]. Wipe the quince clean with a clean, damp cloth, then cut lengthwise in half, using a sharp knife.

Put the quince, cut side up, in a small roasting tray in which they fit snugly, and scatter over the sugar, bay leaves, and vanilla pod (with seeds). Pour over enough verjuice or water to just cover, then seal tightly with foil. Bake on the middle shelf of the oven 1½ hours, then remove the foil and return to the oven a further 30 minutes.

Remove from the oven and pour off the cooking liquor into a small pan. Bring to a boil and let bubble until reduced to a thick syrup consistency, almost like a caramel. Set aside with the baked quince.

For the pastry, it's a good idea to chill the flour in the refrigerator 20 minutes or so before you start. Sift the flour into a bowl. Cut the cold butter into ¼ in [5 mm] slivers, letting them fall into the flour as you cut them. Add the salt and sugar. With your fingertips, work the butter lightly into the dough. You should have a texture like very rough sand. Add the water and mix until the dough just comes together.

Tip the crumby dough onto a large sheet of plastic wrap and lay another piece of plastic wrap on top. Using a rolling pin, roll the dough out between the plastic wrap to a thick disc, then transfer to the refrigerator to rest 15 minutes.

Preheat the oven to 400°F [200°C]. Core each baked quince half, then slice into 4 or 5 wedges. Arrange, skin side down, in a circular pattern over the base of an 8 in [20 cm] springform cake tin. Scatter over the chopped nuts and spoon over 2 Tbsp of the reduced quince cooking liquor.

Unwrap the pastry and place on a lightly floured surface. Roll out very thinly to a large round, about 9½ in [24 cm] in diameter and no thicker than ⅛ in [3 mm]. Trim the edges.

Dot the quince with the butter flakes. Carefully lay the pastry over the top, tucking the edges down inside the rim of the cake tin. Prick the pastry with a fork and sprinkle with the sugar. Bake in the oven 45 minutes until the pastry is dark golden and the juices are bubbling around the edges.

Let stand 10 minutes before carefully inverting and unmolding the tart onto a plate to serve.

Plum upside down cake

*This is a lovely dessert to make from midsummer through to the
end of fall. It looks and smells so inviting as you turn it out, with the
glistening, sweet, juicy fruit nestling in the vanilla-scented sponge.
Use whichever plums are particularly flavorful, or a mixture if you
are spoiled for choice; I find Victoria plums tends to be consistently good.
The cake is best eaten still just slightly warm from the oven, with
a scoop of vanilla ice cream.*

Preheat the oven to 350°F [180°C]. For the topping, put the
butter in a 9 in [23 cm] cake tin (not a loose-bottomed one)
and melt over low heat.

Add the brown sugar and stir until fully dissolved, then swirl
to thoroughly coat the base of the tin. Remove from the heat
and let cool. Halve the plums, remove the stones, and then
cut into quarters. Arrange neatly over the base of the tin.

For the cake mixture, using an electric mixer, beat the butter
and sugar together until pale and light. Add the vanilla
extract, then beat in the egg yolks, one at a time. Sift the
flour, baking powder, and salt together and fold into the
mixture, a third at a time, alternately with the milk (as a rule
of thumb always begin and end with the dry ingredients).

Whisk the egg whites in a separate, clean bowl to stiff peaks,
then gently fold into the mixture, a third at a time.

Pour the mixture into the prepared tin and spread it gently
and evenly over the plums. Bake in the oven 30 minutes or
until the top is golden and the cake is coming away slightly
from the edge of the tin. Remove from the oven and let stand
15 minutes before turning out onto a plate to serve.

Serves 6 to 8

For the topping

⅔ cup [50 g] unsalted butter

⅜ cup [80 g] soft brown
sugar

6 firm ripe plums

For the cake

½ cup [120 g] unsalted butter,
softened

1 ⅛ cups [220 g] superfine
sugar

1 tsp vanilla extract

2 organic free-range medium
eggs, separated

1 ⅔ cups [200 g] all-purpose
flour

2 tsp baking powder

¼ tsp salt

1 ¼ cups [300 ml] whole milk

Apple galette

*I love this simple, classic, understated tart. The secret lies in the crisp,
fine pastry. I like to eat it still slightly warm from the oven with
a scoop of vanilla ice cream. Choose a firm, flavorful dessert apple,
such as Braeburn or Cox's.*

Serves 6 to 8

For the pastry

1 ½ cups [180 g]
all-purpose flour

¼ tsp salt

¾ cup [170 g] chilled
unsalted butter, cut into
small cubes

⅓ cup [80 ml] chilled water

For the almond layer

3 Tbsp ground almonds

3 Tbsp all-purpose flour

⅓ cup [60 g] superfine sugar

For the apple topping

6 to 8 apples (depending
on size)

Pinch of salt

6 Tbsp superfine sugar

1 cup [100 g] shelled walnuts,
roughly chopped

1 ½ Tbsp [20 g] chilled butter,
cut into small flakes

To make the pastry, put the flour, salt, and butter in a food processor and process 5 seconds. The butter should still be visible and in small pieces. Add the water and process 5 seconds more—just enough time for the dough to start holding together. Little pieces of butter should still be visible throughout (this is important to achieve a delicate, flaky pastry). Remove from the machine and lightly gather into a dough with your hands. Form into a ball, flatten slightly, and wrap in plastic wrap. Rest in the refrigerator 30 minutes.

Preheat the oven to 400°F [200°C]. Roll the dough out on a lightly floured cool surface to a large, thin round, about 12 in [30 cm] in diameter. Lift the dough onto a baking sheet.

For the almond layer, toss together the ground almonds, flour, and sugar and scatter over the pastry.

Peel, quarter, and core the apples, then slice into ⅛ in [3 mm] wedges. Place in a bowl and sprinkle with the salt and all but 1 Tbsp of the sugar. Toss well to combine. Taste and add a little more salt if the apple seems too sweet.

Arrange the apples evenly over the pastry, leaving a 2 in [5 cm] clear border. Fold the edges of the pastry up over the fruit, crimping and tucking them gently as you do so. Sprinkle the remaining sugar on top, scatter over the walnuts, and dot with the butter.

Bake in the oven 40 to 45 minutes, or until the pastry is crisp and golden brown. For the best possible flavor and fragrance, eat within 1 hour.

Bitter chocolate and espresso cake

*This cake is wonderfully rich and dense, so a little slice goes a long way.
I like to use chocolate that is dark and smoky in flavor. The
bitter smooth luxuriousness of good coffee adds another dimension
that gives this dessert a very enticing grown-up taste.*

Preheat the oven to 350°F [180°C]. Line an 8 in [20 cm] springform cake tin with heavy-duty foil (so it forms a tight seal) and line with lightly greased baking parchment. Dust the base and sides with flour.

Put the almonds in a blender and pulse until finely ground (the flavor will be better than ready-ground almonds).

Using an electric mixer, whisk the egg yolks and sugar together until pale and almost doubled in volume; this will take around 8 to 10 minutes. The mixture should be thick enough to leave a ribbon trail on the surface when the whisk is lifted. Add the grated chocolate to the mixture with the ground almonds and carefully fold in, along with the coffee.

Whisk the egg whites with the salt in a separate, clean bowl to stiff peaks, then gently fold into the chocolate mixture, a third at a time.

Pour the mixture into the prepared tin. Stand the cake tin in a roasting tray and pour enough hot water around the cake tin to come halfway up the sides. Bake on the middle shelf of the oven 50 minutes or until a skewer inserted into the center comes out clean. Let cool in the tin.

For the topping, put the coffee and chocolate in a bowl over a pan of hot water. Once the chocolate has melted, stir until smooth. Carefully unmold the cake onto a plate and gently prick the surface all over with a skewer. Pour over the glaze and allow to seep in and set on the surface. Serve in slices, with a generous dollop of crème fraîche on the side.

Serves 10

⅔ cup [130 g] unsalted butter, plus extra to grease

All-purpose flour, to dust

1 ⅓ cups [150 g] blanched almonds

7 organic free-range medium eggs, separated, plus 2 extra whites

⅔ cup [130 g] superfine sugar

5¼ oz [150 g] good quality dark chocolate (ideally 70 percent cocoa solids), grated

¼ cup [60 ml] espresso or dark full-bodied coffee (freshly made and cooled)

Pinch of salt

For the glaze

14 Tbsp [200 ml] freshly made rich, dark coffee, cooled

3 oz [80 g] good quality dark chocolate, broken into small pieces

Candied blood orange and white chocolate nougat

At the end of a meal, I enjoy a few bites of something intensely sweet that is also fragrant and delicate, so this beautiful nougat rounds off a meal perfectly for me. It is particularly good made with the candied peel of blood oranges, which we prepare at the restaurant when they are in season. In the summer months, I like to serve the nougat with a tisane made with lemon verbena. (Illustrated overleaf.)

Preheat the oven to 212°F [100°C]. Scatter the pistachios on a baking sheet and roast in the low oven about 20 minutes—to just bring out and intensify their flavor rather than color them. Roasting also firms up their texture to give the nougat a little crunch.

Using a sharp knife, cut the chocolate into roughly ⅜ in [1 cm] pieces and place in the freezer to chill thoroughly. Cut the butter into ⅜ in [1 cm] chunks and place in the refrigerator 20 minutes.

Cut the candied peel into ⅜ to ¾ in [1 to 2 cm] pieces. Strip the leaves from the rosemary and finely chop them. Remove the seeds from the vanilla pod and set aside, along with the rosemary.

Line a shallow 8 x 12 in [20 x 30 cm] baking sheet with 2 sheets of rice paper, making sure you have enough to fold up and cover the sides. I find it helpful to lightly grease the sheet with a little butter first, to help the rice paper stick.

Put the superfine sugar, honey, and glucose into a heavy-based pan and add the water. Put the pan over medium heat to dissolve the sugar and bring to a boil. Once the sugar begins to boil, little crystals may form on the sides of the pan; if so remove these by brushing them with a pastry brush dipped in water. Continue to boil until the syrup reaches 275°F [135°C]; you will need a sugar thermometer to check this.

Makes 60 small pieces

1 ½ cups [150 g] shelled pistachio nuts

7 oz [200 g] good quality white chocolate

⅝ cup [125 g] unsalted butter

5¼ oz [150 g] candied citrus peel (preferably homemade or fine quality store-bought)

4 large, tender rosemary sprigs

1 vanilla pod, split lengthwise

4 sheets of rice paper

2¼ cups [440 g] superfine sugar

4½ oz [125 g] honey

8¾ oz [250 g] liquid glucose

¼ cup [60 ml] water

2 organic free-range medium egg whites

Good pinch of salt

While the syrup mixture is heating, using a mixer fitted with the whisk attachment, slowly whisk the egg whites with a pinch of salt until the eggs break down. Then increase the speed and whisk until soft peaks form.

As soon as the sugar syrup reaches the correct temperature, remove from the heat and let rest 1 minute or so. Then, with the mixer on a low speed, slowly pour the sugar syrup onto the whites as they are whisking. Once it is all added, increase the speed; this will cool the mixture slightly.

When the mixture is still just warm, add the butter pieces, still whisking to break down and incorporate the butter as it moves through the meringue. Once it is evenly combined, add the vanilla and rosemary. Remove the bowl from the machine and fold in the pistachios and candied peel. Lastly stir in the white chocolate pieces. It is important to work quite quickly at this stage as the mixture will begin to set.

Pour the mixture into the prepared tin. Press the 2 remaining sheets of rice paper firmly on top, ensuring any air bubbles are removed. Cover with plastic wrap and chill in the refrigerator at least 4 hours, preferably overnight.

Using a sharp serrated knife, trim the edges of the nougat to neaten, then cut into small slices. Return to the refrigerator until ready to serve.

Canelés de Bordeaux

*I've loved these little fluted pastries since I first came across them as
a cookery student in Paris in the early 1980s. Small and perfectly formed,
their dark bittersweet caramelized crust gives way to a soft filling, laced
with rum and vanilla. Finding them irresistibly elegant, I was determined
to serve them in the Salon at Spring. You will need canelé molds—I use
copper ones that I brought over from France, but these are available
online and at good cook stores.*

Rinse out a heavy-based saucepan with cold water (this helps to prevent the milk from scalding and catching at the sides). Pour the milk into the pan and warm over low heat to 185°F [85°C] (below simmering).

Put the butter, flour, and salt into a food processor and pulse until just combined. Add the sugar and pulse just a couple of seconds to mix. Now add the egg yolks and process until well combined.

With the motor running, slowly pour in the warm milk through the funnel. Once it has all been added, strain the mixture through a fine sieve into a bowl. Stir in the rum and vanilla and let cool, then cover and leave in the refrigerator 24 hours.

A couple of hours before you intend to cook the canelés, brush the inside of the molds generously with oil and place in the freezer.

Preheat the oven to 400°F [200°C]. Stand the canelé molds on a baking sheet and fill them almost to the top with the chilled mixture. Place on the bottom shelf of the oven and bake 1¼ hours until they have formed a dark golden brown crust. Remove from the oven and unmold the canelés as quickly as possible onto a wire rack. Let cool before serving.

Makes 12

2 cups [470 ml] whole milk

⅔ cup [50 g] unsalted butter

⅞ cup [100 g] all-purpose flour

Pinch of salt

¾ cup [150 g] superfine sugar

4 organic free-range medium egg yolks

1 Tbsp dark rum

1 tsp vanilla extract

Sunflower (or other flavorless) oil, to oil the molds

The kitchen

One of the things I found most thrilling about starting a new restaurant was being able to design the kitchen exactly the way I wanted it, within the constraints of the budget, of course. The potential kitchen area at Somerset House was particularly exciting. It was possible to have not one kitchen, but two: one where most of the prep would be done, and another that would be used primarily for service. The main kitchen downstairs even had enough space for a special desserts and pastry section, with a marble top that would run the entire length of one wall. It would also take a large deck oven, in which we could bake bread daily, as well as tarts, and biscuits for cheese.

For me, the finished kitchens at Spring are as close to perfection as they could be. With large windows and high ceilings, both kitchens are light filled and provide plenty of space to be creative in. I wanted to make as much of the food and drinks as possible at the restaurant—so all the breads, butters, soft cheeses, cordials, tonics, and bitters were to come from our kitchen. While the building was being renovated, we worked on these little offerings in a test kitchen until they were just as we wanted them to be.

As always, it is the seasons and our producers who really determine what we cook in the kitchens. We merely decide on combinations that seem to work on the day and go from there. As I see it, our job is to be custodians of that beautiful produce—to do only as much as we need to in order to highlight its natural beauty and flavor. It is a simple, pleasurable way of cooking but one that calls for great care and attention. Much thought and discussion goes into every dish we serve.

ice creams

Langues de chat

*I think it is essential to accompany ice cream with something sharp
and crunchy—something that really snaps and explodes in your mouth
when you bite into it. It should be almost neutral in flavor, certainly
not sweet—it's the texture that's important. These thin little cookies serve
the same purpose as an ice cream cone, albeit not as a container.
I like to make one large sheet and break it into shards to serve,
but you can pipe it and shape it in the more traditional way if you prefer.
These cookies keep well a few days in an airtight container.*

Line 1 large or 2 smaller baking sheets with baking parchment.

Put the butter and powdered sugar in a bowl and beat with a handheld electric mixer until pale and smooth. Sift in half of the flour with the salt and beat well to combine. Repeat with the remaining flour. Add the vanilla and then finally beat in the egg whites.

If you're making one large cookie sheet, paddle the mixture in a thin layer over the lined baking sheet(s), using a palette knife. For individual cookies, spoon the mixture into a piping bag fitted with a ⅜ in [1 cm] nozzle and pipe into 2¾ to 3 in [7 to 8 cm] lengths, leaving 2 in [5 cm] in between to allow room for the cookies to spread during cooking. Put the sheet(s) in the refrigerator 20 minutes or so to allow the dough to firm up.

Preheat the oven to 350°F [180°C]. Take the sheet(s) from the refrigerator and place on the middle shelf of the oven. Bake 8 to 10 minutes if baking a whole sheet, until golden brown around the edges. Allow 6 to 8 minutes for individual cookies.

Remove from the oven and let cool slightly a few minutes, then break the large sheet into pieces (if that's what you have made). Transfer the cookies to a wire rack to cool.

Makes 20 to 25

⅝ cup [125 g] unsalted butter, softened

1 cup [125 g] powdered sugar

1 cup [125 g] all-purpose flour

Pinch of salt

1 tsp vanilla extract

3 organic free-range medium egg whites

Vanilla ice cream

*We serve a scoop of vanilla ice cream with several of our desserts. This
is also the recipe I use for all ice creams that call for a pudding base.
It is straightforward, but calls for patience and care. The pudding
needs to be cooked through to avoid an overpowering eggy flavor and
it must also be thick enough to suspend and hold any flavors to
be added; it takes around 10 minutes to cook over the lowest possible heat.
If you rush this stage by using a higher heat, your pudding is liable to
curdle. I find that I get the best ice cream if I make the pudding the day
before I intend to use it and chill it in the refrigerator overnight.*

*Makes about 4 cups [900 ml]
(12 to 15 scoops)*

2 cups [450 ml] organic heavy
cream

1½ cups [350 ml] organic
whole milk

1 vanilla pod, split in half
lengthwise

6 organic free-range medium
egg yolks

⅔ cup [120 g] superfine
sugar

Pour the cream and milk into a heavy-based pan. Scrape the
seeds from the vanilla pod and add them to the pan with
the empty pod. Slowly bring to just below a simmer. Turn
down the heat to as low as possible and continue to heat
5 minutes, then remove and set aside to infuse 10 minutes.

Meanwhile, whisk the egg yolks and sugar together in a bowl
until pale and thick. Pour on the still-warm milk mixture,
stirring as you do so. Return the pudding to the cleaned pan
and place over very low heat. Stir continuously with a
wooden spoon, using a figure-of-eight movement, until the
pudding is thick enough to coat the back of the spoon and
leaves a channel when you run your finger along it.

Immediately remove from the heat and strain through a
fine sieve into a bowl. Let cool, then cover and chill in the
refrigerator overnight.

The next day, churn the pudding in an ice-cream machine
until thick and creamy, according to the manufacturer's
instructions. It is now ready to serve as a simple vanilla ice
cream, or to transform into a flavored ice cream (see below
and pages 183 to 9). Store in an airtight container in the
freezer until needed.

Mango ice cream Prepare the vanilla ice cream base as above
and chill overnight. Peel, stone, and slice 2 ripe mangoes
(preferably Alphonso) and place in a blender. Add a squeeze
of lime juice and purée until really smooth. Fold the mango
purée into the ice cream base and churn as above.

Burned caramel, ginger, and chocolate ice cream

For years I've attempted to make a really rich, bitter chocolate ice cream. It has always proved difficult and frustrating, as the more chocolate you add, the less the ice cream wants to freeze. This idea stems from an intensely rich chocolate mousse with ginger caramel syrup we served at Petersham, which was always finished off with an overly large scoop of buttery Jersey cream. Here I've essentially rolled it all into one and churned it into an ice cream.

Prepare the vanilla ice cream base as described on page 183 and chill thoroughly overnight.

The next day, for the caramel, place the sugar and ⅝ cup [150 ml] of the water in a small heavy-based saucepan over low heat. Bring to a simmer, stirring once or twice with a wooden spoon to help dissolve the sugar. Once it has all dissolved, increase the heat and allow the syrup to bubble to a rich amber caramel. This will take about 10 minutes and requires a certain amount of bravery because in order to get a really intense flavor you must almost smell the burn.

As soon as you can smell the darkness of the sugar, remove the pan from the heat and carefully pour in the remaining 1 cup [250 ml] water, standing back as it will sizzle and bubble. Return to the heat and stir continuously to dissolve the caramel. Once fully dissolved, remove from the heat and add the sliced ginger.

Stir the chocolate pieces into the caramel—they will melt gently in the heat. Finally, sift in the cocoa powder. Strain the mixture through a fine sieve onto the chilled pudding and fold through.

Transfer to your ice-cream machine and churn until the ice cream is thick and creamy, according to the manufacturer's instructions. Store in an airtight container in the freezer until ready to serve.

Serves 8 to 10 (or more, depending on portion size)

For the vanilla ice cream base

2 cups [450 ml] organic heavy cream

1½ cups [350 ml] organic whole milk

1 vanilla pod, split in half lengthwise

6 organic free-range medium egg yolks

⅔ cup [120 g] superfine sugar

For the burned caramel flavoring

1¼ cup [250 g] superfine sugar

1⅔ cups [400 ml] water

2 in [5 cm] thumb of fresh ginger, peeled and finely sliced

5¼ oz [150 g] good quality dark chocolate, broken into small pieces

1 Tbsp dark unsweetened cocoa powder

Roasted strawberry and balsamic ice cream

*I think of strawberry ice cream as summer in a mouthful—it's
so deliciously bright, sharp, and sweet. This recipe is slightly different.
The addition of balsamic vinegar and the gentle roasting of the
strawberries turns it into something altogether more grown up and
elegant, with a mellow fullness to its flavor. Plump, ripe strawberries
and good quality aged balsamic are absolutely essential.*

*Serves 8 to 10 (or more,
depending on portion size)*

For the vanilla ice cream base

2 cups [450 ml] organic heavy cream

1½ cups [350 ml] organic whole milk

1 vanilla pod, split in half lengthwise

6 organic free-range medium egg yolks

⅔ cup [120 g] superfine sugar

For the roasted strawberries

14 oz [400 g] ripe strawberries (in season)

1 Tbsp superfine sugar

Pinch of sea salt

3 Tbsp aged balsamic vinegar

Prepare the vanilla ice cream base as described on page 183 and chill thoroughly overnight.

The next day, preheat the oven to 320°F [160°C]. Wash and hull the strawberries and put in a bowl. Sprinkle with the sugar and a little pinch of salt, drizzle over the balsamic vinegar, and toss together gently, using your hands, to ensure the strawberries are all lightly coated. Transfer to a roasting sheet and place on the middle shelf of the oven. Roast 5 to 6 minutes; the strawberries should still be firm enough to hold their shape.

Let the roasted strawberries to cool completely, then transfer to a blender and blitz to a purée.

Fold the strawberry purée into the chilled pudding base, then transfer to your ice-cream machine and churn until thick and creamy, according to the manufacturer's instructions. Store the ice cream in an airtight container in the freezer until ready to serve.

Blueberry, lemon, and mascarpone ice cream

This ice cream has a wonderfully nostalgic flavor. It reminds me of something sweet from my childhood, although I can't quite put my finger on exactly what that was. It has a lovely texture too.

Prepare the vanilla ice cream base as described on page 183 and chill thoroughly overnight.

The next day, put the blueberries into a saucepan with the sugar, lemon zest, and a splash of water. Put over medium heat and bring almost to a simmer, then turn down the heat and cook until the blueberries are soft and falling apart, about 10 minutes. The berries will have released a certain amount of liquid, creating a dark, slightly viscous syrup. The lemon zest should also be tender and translucent. At this point, remove the pan from the heat and let cool.

Once cool, transfer the blueberries, softened lemon zest, and syrup to a blender and purée until smooth.

Put the mascarpone into a bowl and stir in the puréed blueberry syrup, then fold in the chilled pudding base. Transfer to your ice-cream machine and churn until thick and creamy, according to the manufacturer's instructions. Store the ice cream in an airtight container in the freezer until ready to serve.

Serves 8 to 10 (or more, depending on portion size)

For the vanilla ice cream base

2 cups [450 ml] organic heavy cream

1 ½ cups [350 ml] organic whole milk

1 vanilla pod, split in half lengthwise

6 organic free-range medium egg yolks

⅔ cup [120 g] superfine sugar

For the blueberry flavoring

10½ oz [300 g] blueberries

5⅓ Tbsp [80 g] superfine sugar

Finely pared zest of 1 lemon (in one strip)

3½ oz [100 g] mascarpone

Walnut and chestnut honey ice cream

*Make this ice cream in the early months of the fall when young walnuts
become available. Sometimes referred to as "wet walnuts," they have
a soft, creamy texture and a delicious sweet flavor; their skin is flaky and
free of bitterness. Buy only the amount that you need—in their shells—
as they are very perishable. I like to include as many walnuts as possible,
to give the ice cream plenty of crunch and texture, but you can use less
if you prefer. Chestnut honey has a pronounced flavor—slightly malty and
almost bitter. It lends a distinctive note, but feel free to use
a lighter, fragrant honey, such as acacia, if you prefer.*

*Serves 8 to 10 (or more,
depending on portion size)*

For the vanilla ice cream base

2 cups [450 ml] organic heavy
cream

1 ½ cups [350 ml] organic
whole milk

1 vanilla pod, split in half
lengthwise

6 organic free-range medium
egg yolks

⅔ cup [120 g] superfine
sugar

*For the walnut and honey
flavoring*

2¾ cups [300 g] freshly
shelled young walnuts

2 Tbsp chestnut honey

Prepare the vanilla ice cream base as described on page 183 and chill thoroughly overnight.

The next day, preheat the oven to 350°F [180°C]. Put the walnuts on a baking sheet and warm in the oven to slightly accentuate both their flavor and bite—no more than a couple of minutes, as you are not looking to color them. Remove and let cool slightly, then chop roughly or pound coarsely using a mortar and pestle.

Spoon the honey into the chilled pudding base and stir well to combine. Transfer to your ice-cream machine and churn until almost set, according to the manufacturer's instructions, generally about 20 minutes. Add the walnuts and churn a couple more minutes, just to distribute them evenly. Store in an airtight container in the freezer until ready to serve.

Campari, pomegranate, and clementine sorbet

*This is a sharp, clean, sophisticated sorbet, gloriously bright in color
and wonderfully refreshing. A lovely light dessert to round off a hearty
winter's meal. I like to serve it with crisp dessert cookies, such as the
langues de chat on page 180.*

Chop the lemon roughly, including the skin; discard the pips. Put the chopped lemon into a food processor along with the sugar and purée until the lemon is smooth. Add the Campari and clementine juice and pulse to combine.

Transfer the mixture to a bowl, add the pomegranate juice and stir well to combine. Pour into your ice-cream machine and churn until frozen, according to the manufacturer's instructions. Serve the sorbet straightaway or transfer to a suitable container and place in the freezer until ready to use; for the best flavor, use within a week.

Serves 10

1 lemon (unwaxed)

2 cups [400 g] superfine sugar

14 Tbsp [200 ml] Campari

Juice of 5 clementines

4½ cups [1 L] fresh pomegranate juice

Ricotta, pistachio, and chocolate ice cream sandwich

The idea for the Salon at Spring came from a desire to have "a little bar of treats," with a short menu that would offer something quite different from the main restaurant. To me, this is almost the perfect sweet treat.

Makes 20 to 25

For the sponge

⅓ cup [70 g] unsalted butter, melted and cooled, plus extra to grease

1 ½ cups [190 g] all-purpose flour, plus extra to dust

6 organic free-range eggs

¾ cup [150 g] golden superfine sugar

½ tsp vanilla extract

1 tsp orange flower water

For the ice cream

10 ½ oz [300 g] mild-flavored honey (I like orange blossom)

2 cups [500 ml] milk

1 vanilla pod, split in half lengthwise

4 organic free-range medium egg yolks

5⅓ Tbsp [80 g] golden superfine sugar

Finely grated zest of 1 orange

1 Tbsp orange flower water

15¾ oz [450 g] ricotta

3½ oz [100 g] good quality dark chocolate, finely chopped

½ cup [50 g] shelled pistachio nuts, skinned and finely chopped

½ cup [50 g] candied peel (ideally homemade cedro or blood orange peel, or use good quality store-bought citrus peel), finely chopped

First make the ice cream. Bring the honey to a boil in a medium saucepan and cook 3 to 4 minutes until it starts to caramelize. Remove from the heat and let cool slightly, then carefully pour in the milk, stirring. Add the vanilla pod (with seeds), return to the heat, and whisk to combine, then set aside to infuse.

Whisk the egg yolks and sugar together in a bowl until pale and creamy, then add the orange zest and orange flower water. Pour onto the still-warm honey and milk mixture, whisking as you do so. Return the pudding to the cleaned pan and stir over very low heat with a wooden spoon, using a figure-of-eight movement, until it is thick enough to coat the back of the spoon. Strain through a fine sieve into a bowl.

Put the ricotta in a blender and process briefly until smooth. Add a third of the pudding and blitz to combine, then pour the ricotta mixture into the remaining pudding in the bowl and stir well to combine. Let cool, then chill in the refrigerator a couple of hours.

For the sponge, preheat the oven to 350°F [180°C]. Butter and flour a 9 in [23 cm] square cake tin. Using an electric mixer, beat the eggs, sugar, and vanilla extract together until the mixture is pale and has doubled in volume, about 5 minutes. Sift and carefully fold in the flour, a third at a time. Finally, fold in the orange flower water and melted butter.

Pour the mixture into the prepared tin and spread it evenly, using a spatula. Bake in the oven about 8 to 10 minutes until golden and the center of the sponge springs back when lightly pressed. Let cool in the tin, then turn out and slice horizontally into two layers.

Transfer the chilled ice cream to your ice-cream machine and churn until set. Fold in the chopped chocolate, nuts, and candied peel.

Lay the bottom cake layer on a board lined with baking parchment. Spoon the ice cream on top of the cake and smooth evenly using a palette knife. Sandwich together with the other cake layer and press down gently and evenly. Lay another sheet of parchment on top, then place in the freezer 2 to 3 hours.

To serve, slice the cake into slim fingers. Lovely with espresso.

The table

I was really excited by the idea of creating the table top at Spring. I approached it in terms of thinking how the food could be framed and showcased—like a painting, I suppose. I wanted it to be clean and white, simple and thoughtful, and I wanted the tables to be clothed.

During the months of building it seemed that cloths were being removed from restaurant tables everywhere, while I was searching for just the right cloths to put on ours! I was convinced that a soft, white linen cloth with a slight texture would feel cool and fresh—and most importantly, relaxed. It took a while to find just the right material, not least because it was essential that the napkins were made of the same fabric. They needed to be large and generous, too.

As for the cutlery, I wanted this to have a contemporary feel and to be relatively heavy and solid to hold—certainly not in any way flimsy. After much searching, we chose an English design from David Mellor.

I had always known the plates would be white, round, and plain. Food has such alluring, natural colors and shapes that, to me, are best appreciated on a simple background. Size is important too. Small plates can make everything look cramped, but if plates are too big the food can look serious and imposing. I like enough space and air around food to allow it to feel at ease and unfurl on the plate.

I wanted to bring some color to the table too, in a light, transparent way. Recycled glasses worked perfectly—the green glass reflecting light softly on the white cloth. For cocktails and cordials, I opted for beautiful colored glasses from Murano in Venice.

Finally, Brickett Davda, an English ceramicist, made us little bowls glazed in contrasting colors of tobacco, olive green, and smoky gray for the homemade butter and sea salt that would sit on every table. I wanted the table to feel personal and considered, but relaxed and easy.

drinks

Lime cordial

*I grew up on lime cordial—we always had a bottle in our pantry at home—
we drank it really cold over lots of ice with a splash or two of bitters
and soda water. It was the closest thing we ever came to drinking
carbonated drinks at home. My mother still makes a large pitcher of
it whenever I visit. I now make my own lime cordial—I prefer it—it is
sharper, cleaner, fresher, and tastes more truly of the fruit. It works
beautifully with a drop or two of bitters (see page 211).*

Makes about 4½ cups [1 L]

10 limes

4½ cups [1 L] water

2¼ cups [450 g] golden
superfine sugar

2 tsp citric acid

Crushed ice, to serve

Using a vegetable peeler, finely pare the zest from the limes.
Now squeeze the juice, strain, and set aside.

Put the water and lime zest into a saucepan and bring to a
boil. Add the sugar and citric acid, stir well to combine, and
continue to boil 3 minutes. Add the lime juice and heat
another 2 minutes. Take off the heat and let cool.

Strain the cordial into sterilized jars, discarding the lime
zest. Put in the refrigerator 24 hours or so. I find it tastes
better if allowed to sit for a day or so before using.

Put plenty of crushed ice into a pitcher and pour on the
cordial until the pitcher is about three-quarters full. Top
up with water to taste and stir well, then serve.

Cucumber and lime cordial

Clean, clear, and soothing in flavor, this cordial is beautiful on a hot summer's day. It has a wonderfully invigorating and refreshing quality. Like the cordials that follow, it is best served as an apéritif, rather than with the meal. It can also form the base for a delicious Prosecco cocktail.

I think the balance is just about right with the quantity of lime suggested here, but you can add a little more, or use less as you prefer. And if you grow lemon verbena in your backyard, add a few leaves to the sugar syrup. Look for cucumbers that are firm and heavy for their size, without any bruises or blemishes.

Start by making the sugar syrup. Put the sugar and water into a heavy-based pan and place over medium heat. Bring to a boil, stirring once or twice to help dissolve the sugar. Once the sugar syrup has come to a boil, turn down the heat slightly and simmer for 5 minutes. Remove from the heat and let cool.

Rinse the cucumbers, pat dry, and put in a blender or food processor. Blitz until smooth, then pass through a sieve into a bowl, pressing down on the cucumber flesh in the sieve as you do so to extract as much juice as possible.

Stir in half of the cooled sugar syrup, then taste and add a little more if you think it needs it. Add the lime juice and stir really well to combine.

Put plenty of crushed ice into a pitcher and pour on the cordial until the pitcher is three-quarters full. Top up with water and stir well. Add the mint sprigs and let the cordial sit 1 or 2 minutes to allow the flavors to mingle, then serve.

Makes about 3⅛ cups [750 ml]

1⅛ cups [225 g] golden superfine sugar

2⅛ cups [500 ml] water

4 small cucumbers (or 1 large one)

Juice of 3 limes

To serve

Crushed ice

5 to 6 mint sprigs

Lovage and fennel seed cordial

The idea for this cordial came from Will, a brilliant young cook who works for me, from the time he spent at Chez Panisse in Berkeley. After service one warm evening, the staff poured a hot sugar syrup over lovage and drank it there and then. The concept intrigued me! The fresh, intensely peppery flavor of lovage, so reminiscent of celery, served in the form of a drink . . . what could that possibly taste like? I plucked some sprigs from a pot in the garden and tried it for myself, there and then. I was surprised and pleased by the taste. I have since added crushed fennel seeds, which give the final taste a little body and depth.

To make the sugar syrup, put the sugar and water into a heavy-based pan and place over medium heat. Bring to a boil, stirring once or twice to help dissolve the sugar. When it comes to a boil, turn down the heat slightly and simmer 5 to 10 minutes until the syrup thickens slightly and becomes viscous. Remove from the heat.

Put the lovage sprigs in a bowl and pour over the warm sugar syrup. Crush the fennel seeds coarsely, using a mortar and pestle, then add to the bowl. Leave to infuse and cool.

You can either serve the cordial straightaway or strain it into a sterilized jar, seal, and refrigerate. It will keep happily in the refrigerator for a couple of weeks.

To serve, put plenty of crushed ice into a pitcher or directly into glasses. Pour on the cordial until about three-quarters full (add as much or as little cordial as you like—according to preference). Add the lime juice and top up with sparkling water to taste. Stir well and serve.

Makes about 3⅛ cups [750 ml]

1¼ cups [225 g] golden superfine sugar

2⅛ cups [500 ml] water

3 to 4 lovage sprigs

1 tsp fennel seeds

To serve

Crushed ice

Juice of ½ lime

Sparkling water

Lemon barley water

This is a lovely soothing, yet thirst-quenching, cordial. Traditionally given to calm sore stomachs, it has rather gone out of fashion except in the form of the very sweet store-bought variety. You can add other flavorings to it besides barley, lemon, and honey—lemon verbena or ginger would work well and I have come across it in Asia with the addition of aromatic pandan leaves.

Don't discard the barley. Stir through a vegetable soup, or dress it simply with a little olive oil and lemon juice and add to a salad.

Rinse the barley several times under cold running water, then tip into a saucepan and add the water. Bring to a boil over medium heat, then immediately reduce the heat to a simmer and cook until the barley is tender; this will take about 35 minutes. Drain, reserving the cooking water, and set the cooked barley aside.

Return the cooking water to a clean pan, add the honey, and heat gently, stirring, just to dissolve. Remove from the heat and let cool.

Add the lemon juice and serve over ice.

Makes 5 to 6½ cups [1.2 to 1.5 L]

7 oz [200 g] pearl barley

2½ qt [2.5 L] water

3 Tbsp light-flavored honey, such as acacia

Juice of 1 lemon

Ice, to serve

Quince, ginger, and bay cordial

*I started making this lovely earthy, early winter cordial many years ago.
In fact, it was one of the first cordials I attempted. Like many good
things, it came about from a by-product of something else: quince paste.
To make this paste, quinces are first cooked slowly in sugar syrup, which
is then discarded. Throwing away this beautiful dark amber liquid has
always seemed an awful waste to me, so I set about turning it into a drink.
The bay and ginger, which lend a slightly peppery warmth, were later
additions. This cordial keeps well in the refrigerator a couple of weeks.*

Makes about 4½ cups [1 L]

6 quinces

1 ¾ cups [350 g] golden
superfine sugar

About 7 ½ cups [1.8 L] water

2 in [5 cm] piece of fresh
ginger, peeled and roughly
chopped

4 bay leaves, plus a sprig or
two of leaves to serve

Juice of 1 lemon

To serve

Crushed ice

Sparkling water

Using a clean, dry cloth, wipe the quinces all over to remove the bristly down that often covers the outer layer of skin. Put the fruit in a large saucepan, add the sugar, and pour over enough water to cover. Add the ginger and bay. Bring to a boil over medium heat, stirring once or twice to help dissolve the sugar.

Turn the heat down and simmer until the quinces are tender and falling apart, topping up the water from time to time as necessary during cooking. As they cook, the quinces will slowly turn from the palest green to the most glorious burned amber color. You will need to be patient, as the cooking process will take a couple of hours.

Once cooked, remove from the heat and lift the fruit out into a bowl, using a slotted spoon. Don't discard the poached quinces—either serve them just as they are, or with thick, creamy Greek-style yogurt, a few chopped pecans, and a drizzle or two of honey—perfect for breakfast.

For the cordial, let the quince syrup cool, then pass through a strainer into a pitcher or bowl and add the lemon juice.

To serve, put plenty of crushed ice into a pitcher or directly into glasses. Pour on the cordial and top up with sparkling water. Stir well, add a sprig of bay leaves and serve. Alternatively, add a little cordial to a glass of sparkling wine.

White peach and lemon verbena

*This beautiful drink takes me back to my teenage years in Sydney, to
Bill and Toni's, where I used to drink coffee and hang out with my friends.
Just beyond the coffee machine were little glass bottles of wonderful Italian
soft drinks, such as chinotto and fruit juices, all lined up in a row. The
peach nectar, a thick, velvety, ambrosial nectar, was my favorite.*

*Here, I've flavored fresh peach juice with lemon verbena. I love this
herb's clear, sharp, citrusy flavor and use it in many desserts and drinks.
Look for peaches that are ripe without any bruises.*

Makes about 3 cups [700 ml]

6 ripe peaches

⅞ cup [180 g] golden
superfine sugar

4½ cups [1 L] water

6 lemon verbena sprigs

2 little squeezes of lime juice

To serve

Crushed ice

Sparkling water

Wash the peaches and pat dry. Put the sugar and water into a heavy-based medium pan and add the sprigs of lemon verbena. Place over medium heat and bring to a boil, stirring every so often to help the sugar dissolve. Once the sugar syrup has come to a boil, turn the heat down slightly and simmer 5 minutes.

Add the peaches to the pan and cook until tender when pierced with a knife; this will take about 8 minutes. Remove the pan from the heat and let cool.

When the peaches are cool enough to handle, lift them out of the syrup and peel away the skins. Chop the flesh roughly, discarding the stones. Discard the verbena sprigs from the sugar syrup.

Now purée the peaches with the poaching syrup in a blender until smooth. It is best to do this in a couple of batches, adding a little squeeze of lime juice to each batch.

Put plenty of crushed ice into a pitcher and add the peach purée. I like to dilute it with a little gently carbonated water.

Grenadine

*As I was growing up, a glass of sickly sweet pink lemonade was a real
treat on special occasions. It felt glamorous and exciting and it signified
that there was something to celebrate. I think it must have included
a little grenadine, although it tasted nothing like real grenadine, which
is made using fresh pomegranates. This recipe is far less sweet than
the commercial variety. The color of deep magenta, it has a wonderfully
sharp, floral vibrancy. I have added a little rhubarb and rose water
to give it an added depth.*

*Makes about 1 ¼ cups
[300 ml]*

3 sticks rhubarb

2 cups [400 g] golden
superfine sugar

2 large pomegranates

2 tsp rose water

A few drops of lemon juice

Sparkling water, to serve
(optional)

Wash the rhubarb and slice into 2 in [5 cm] pieces. Put in a
pan with ½ cup [100 g] of the sugar and pour on just enough
water to cover. Put over low heat and cook, stirring once or
twice to help dissolve the sugar, until the rhubarb is tender
and just falling apart. Remove from the heat and pass
through a sieve, pressing on the fruit as you do so to extract
as much juice as possible.

Slice the pomegranates in half and press the cut sides down
onto a juicer to extract the juice. Strain the pomegranate
juice into a clean pan and add the rest of the sugar and the
rhubarb juice.

Put over medium heat and bring to a boil, stirring once or
twice to help dissolve the sugar. Lower the heat and simmer
5 minutes. Remove from the heat and let cool, then add the
rose water and a little squeeze of lemon juice. The grenadine
is now ready to use as required, or serve diluted with
sparkling water to taste.

Tonic

Once we started delving into making drinks, it seemed only natural to come up with our own tonic recipe. Quinine, which is derived from the bark of the cinchona tree, gives tonic its characteristic bitter quality. Malic acid, another ingredient, is a form of citric acid with a not unpleasant sour flavor; it helps to preserve cordials and also gives them a clarity of color. I ordered some cinchona bark and malic acid online and began to experiment. There are some very good tonics on the market, so I'm not suggesting it is necessary to make your own, but this one will give you a particularly special gin and tonic.

Bring the water to a boil in a pan, then add the cinchona bark. Immediately take off the heat and add the lemongrass, orange, lime, and grapefruit zests. Set aside to infuse 20 minutes.

Strain the infused water through a fine sieve into a bowl, discarding the flavorings. Add the honey, malic acid, ground allspice, and orange flower water. Stir to encourage the honey to dissolve. Pour into a sterilized jar and keep in the refrigerator.

To use, simply add 3 parts soda water to 1 part tonic. We have found that the perfect gin and tonic is made with 3 parts soda water, 2 parts gin, and 1 part tonic syrup. It is also very nice if you add a splash of Campari!

Makes about 4½ cups [1 L]
4½ cups [1 L] water
4 tsp cinchona bark
1 lemongrass stalk, bruised
Finely grated zest of 1 orange
Finely grated zest of 1 lime
Finely grated zest of 1 pink grapefruit
13¼ oz [375 g] raw honey (I use acacia)
1½ tsp malic acid
1 tsp ground allspice
1 tsp orange flower water
Soda water, to serve

Bitters

Bitters give atmosphere, depth, and character to drinks. If a cocktail seems to be lacking something, bitters is often the missing element. Just a few drops will add the complexity that a cocktail needs. Bitters is essentially high-proof alcohol infused with various different barks, such as gentian and angostura. This recipe belongs much more to Jack Lewens, our sommelier. I set him a task last year to create the best tonic and bitter recipes—both recipes are the result of his laborious experimentations.

Makes 3 cups [700 ml]

1 lemon

1 blood orange

1 ½ in [4 cm] piece of fresh ginger

1 tsp black peppercorns

1 cinnamon stick

5 allspice berries

4 cloves

30 drops of gentian extract

3 cups [700 ml] grain alcohol

Finely pare the zest from the lemon and orange, using a vegetable peeler; it is essential to avoid the pith, as it will add too much bitterness to the end result. Peel and finely slice the ginger.

Put the citrus zests, ginger, spices, and gentian extract into a sterilized jar, pour over the alcohol, and seal tightly. Leave to stand 2 weeks at room temperature, shaking the jar every other day.

Strain the alcohol, discarding all the flavoring ingredients. The bitters is now ready to use. It is best used within the first month or so of making but it can be stored up to 1 year.

Fig liqueur

*As you walk into Spring and cast your eye over the marble bar at the
end of the restaurant you will notice carboys of brightly colored liquids.
Two months prior to opening, I asked Jonas, a young, enthusiastic barman
who had recently joined us, to create some seasonal liqueurs.
He fashioned a laboratory in our office kitchen and set about the challenge
energetically, often arriving with bounty he had foraged from his local
heath. One morning he brought in a bundle of leaves from the fig tree
in his yard. This beautiful pale green liqueur is the product.*

Makes about 5¼ qt [5 L]

40 fig leaves

2 qt [2 L] Chase gin (high
alcohol content)

2 qt [2 L] water

3 lb [1.5 kg] superfine sugar

Crushed ice, to serve

Wash the fig leaves well and pat them dry. Put two-thirds of the leaves into a carboy or other large glass vessel. Pour over the gin and shake well to combine. Leave, uncovered, to infuse 24 hours, then remove and discard the leaves. Strain the liquid through a muslin-lined sieve into a clean container and add half of the water.

Pour the rest of the water into a saucepan and add the sugar. Put over medium heat and bring to just below a boil, stirring to dissolve the sugar. Remove from the heat.

Put the remaining fig leaves into a blender with a little of the sugar syrup and blend until the leaves are very fine. Add to the remaining sugar syrup. Leave to infuse overnight, then strain through a muslin-lined sieve into a clean pan. Once again, bring to just below a boil, then remove from the heat and let cool completely.

Add the fig syrup to the gin mixture and stir well. Pour into a sterilized carboy and store in a cool dark place 1 or 2 weeks before using.

Serve in beautiful, small glasses, with plenty of crushed ice.

Bicerin

*I first had this darkly bitter and intoxicating little drink sitting in the
fading fall light at Caffé Mulassano in Turin in 2006. It was the first time I
had visited this beautiful city—there to attend Terra Madre, the Slow Food
Symposium for the first time. The effect this event had on me is
etched in my memory. My awareness and thinking about food changed so
much over that weekend and the warmth I feel for this little drink is caught
up in that whirl of feelings. I love its elegance and depth of flavor.*

*Good quality coffee is essential—ideally an espresso blend. If you do not
own an espresso machine, use a cafetière or Bialetti coffee maker as I do.*

Break the chocolate into pieces and put in a heatproof bowl over a pan of gently simmering water, making sure the bottom of the bowl is not in contact with the water. Put over low heat and allow the chocolate to melt, without stirring, in the heat of the steam.

Meanwhile, whip the cream to soft peaks and fold in the vanilla extract together with powdered sugar to taste, carefully but thoroughly.

Once the chocolate has melted, remove the bowl from the pan and stir the hot coffee into the melted chocolate. The texture should be rich but not so thick that it does not pour easily into a glass. Pour into glasses and spoon the vanilla cream on top. Serve at once.

Serves 6 to 8

10½ oz [300 g] good quality dark chocolate (70 percent cocoa solids)

7 Tbsp [100 ml] heavy cream

¼ tsp vanilla extract

1 Tbsp powdered sugar, sifted, or to taste

1 ¼ cup [300 ml] freshly brewed espresso coffee

The opening

Finally, the heavy work was finished. The wallpaper was hung meticulously, the lights were suspended from the high ceilings, and Emma Peascod's beautiful painted glass was in place above the bar. It began to look like the room I had imagined so clearly. The final element to be positioned was Valeria Nascimento's ceramic blossoms, on the large expanses of wall either side of the three huge arched windows facing onto Lansuperfine Place. Every one of the 4,800 ceramic petals needed to be suspended from a nail in the wall by a magnet. Arduous and painstaking, the work took almost four days to complete. The end result is one of my favorite elements of Spring; I find it beautiful, uplifting, and serene.

The tables were now in position, the chairs tucked under, and the cloths were laid. For months I had tried to picture how those tables would look when the candles were lit. Throughout the project, I had shed tears only twice—with frustration and impatience when things weren't going quite to plan. But at that moment, as the light fell from the early October sky and the candles were lit, I cried with sheer joy, pride, and a tremendous sense of relief that we had finally achieved our goal.

The past two years spent developing Spring had been challenging and creative but I had missed the pace and camaraderie of the restaurant kitchen. I longed to be back, surrounded by inquisitive and like-minded cooks. I missed the excitement of the changing seasons, the arrival each morning of boxes of beautiful produce to be smelled, touched, and marveled over, and the happy discussions that followed as we settled on what to do with them.

Of course, I was nervous about the opening of the restaurant and cooking again, but the kitchen is the place where I feel most confident—most at ease and most myself. As soon as the kitchens were up and running, and the flames of the stoves were lit, I felt a happiness seep through me. Once again, I would be doing the thing that I loved more than anything—running a restaurant kitchen, this time in the heart of London.